THE EFFECT OF A NORTH AMERICAN FREE TRADE AGREEMENT ON THE COMMONWEALTH CARIBBEAN

THE EFFECT OF A NORTH AMERICAN FREE TRADE AGREEMENT ON THE COMMONWEALTH CARIBBEAN

Jennifer Hosten-Craig

The Edwin Mellen Press
Lewiston/Queenston/Lampeter

Library of Congress Cataloging-in-Publication Data

Hosten-Craig, Jennifer.
The effect of a North American Free Trade agreement on the Commonwealth Caribbean / Jennifer Hosten-Craig.
p. cm.
Includes bibliographical references.
ISBN 0-7734-9554-1
1. Caribbean, English-speaking--Foreign economic relations--North America. 2. North America--Foreign economic relations--Caribbean, English-speaking. 3. Free trade--Caribbean, English-speaking. 4. Free trade--North America. 5. Caribbean, English-speaking--Economic integration. I. Title.
HF1506.5.Z4N674 1992
337.729--dc20 92-14030
CIP

A CIP catalog record for this book is available from The British Library.

The Edwin Mellen Press
P.O. Box 450
Lewiston, NY 14092
USA

The Edwin Mellen Press
Box 67
Queenston, Ontario
CANADA L0S 1L0

The Edwin Mellen Press, Ltd.
Lampeter, Dyfed, wales
UNITED KINGDOM SA48 7DY

Printed in the United States of America

In loving memory of my mother, Phyllis Hosten.

TABLE OF CONTENTS

LIST OF ILLUSTRATIONS

LIST OF ABBREVIATIONS

ACP	Africa, Caribbean and Pacific
CARIBCAN	Canada-Caribbean trade agreement
CARICOM	Caribbean Community
CARIFTA	Caribbean Free Trade Agreement
CBERA	Caribbean Basin Recovery Act
CBI	Caribbean Basin Initiative
CDB	Caribbean Development Bank
CEPAL	Commission for Latin America and the Caribbean
CET	Common External Tariff
CMT	Cut, Make and Trim
DCLs	Designated Consultation Levels
EAI	Enterprise for the Americas Initiative
ECLAC	Economic Commission for Latin America and the Caribbean
EEC	European Economic Community
FTA	Free Trade Agreement
FTZs	Free trade zones
GALs	Guaranteed Access Levels
GATT	General Agreement on Tariffs and Trade
GPT	General Preferential Tariff
IDB	Inter-American Development Bank
IMF	International Monetary Fund
LDCs	Less developed countries
LOMÉ	Agreement between EEC and ACP states
MDCs	More developed countries
MFA	Multi Fibre Arrangement

MNCs	Multinational corporations
NAC	National Advisory Council
NAFTA	North American Free Trade Agreement
NGOs	Non government organizations
NT	National Treatment
OECS	Organization of Eastern Caribbean States
SA	Structural adjustment
SAP	Special Access Program
SLs	Special limits
US	United States
UWI	University of the West Indies
WAND	Women and development

Acknowledgements

I wish to thank all those who assisted me in the completion of this study. In particular, I would like to thank the Canadian Bureau for International Education (CBIE) and the Canadian International Development Agency (CIDA) for making the research possible. I also wish to thank Professor Vincent Seymour Wilson for his advice and encouragement. I am particularly grateful for the generosity and honesty of those interviewed, without whom this study would not have been possible. Special thanks are due to Connie Harvey and Suzanne Lapierre for providing invaluable editing and for working overtime to help me meet deadlines. Last, but by no means least, I wish to thank my husband, David, and children, Sophia and Beau, for putting up with my absences from home, as well as the 'constant paper' over the past months and for their never-failing support.

Foreword

The traditional economic order throughout the industrialized world is under tremendous strain. In the past few years we have seen sweeping changes in the global competitive environment--rapid growth of trade and investment, more open competition, the globalization of industries, shifting corporate strategies, rapid technological changes, and increased economic integration among various countries.

More particularly in North America we have been privy to a vigorous debate and final sanctioning of the Free Trade Agreement with the United States. At the present time this debate continues as North America (United States, Canada and Mexico) contemplates an imminent signing of a North American Free Trade Agreement. What implications this contemplated event might have on Canada's smaller trading partners in the Commonwealth Caribbean is the subject matter of this publication.

Mrs. Jennifer Hosten-Craig has much to say about the prospects facing the islands in the sun. I will not steal her thunder. Suffice to state here that she spent considerable time in Ottawa, Washington, Mexico and seven of the thirteen Caribbean Common Market or CARICOM states intensively interviewing principals involved and compiling the relevant information and statistics to write this volume. The result is an excellent perspective on what Caribbean political and social elites think of the impending changes in the world economic order with which they must deal.

Mrs. Hosten-Craig brings to this project an empathy and passionate interest in the subject matter. She is a child of the Caribbean who has never forgotten her "roots". Additionally she has represented the Caribbean in many different capacities, chief amongst them being High Commissioner for Grenada in Canada between 1978-1981. This interest, coupled with her passionate concern for the people in the Caribbean, makes this document a must read for those interested in the economic, political and social order of the region. It has something to say and it says it well.

V. Seymour Wilson
President, The Canadian Political Science Association and
Professor of Political Science
Carleton University

Introduction

The challenge posed by a possible North American Free Trade Agreement (NAFTA) is considered to be a significant one for Caribbean countries. The purpose of this study is to examine the likely effects of a NAFTA on the Caribbean. In this context the focus will be on the Commonwealth or English-speaking Caribbean countries that are members of the Caribbean Common Market (CARICOM).[1]

It is hypothesized in this study that NAFTA and the Enterprise for the Americas Initiative (EAI), a new initiative by the American administration to extend elements of free trade to the Caribbean and Latin America, could seriously undermine existing trading agreements between the United States (US), Canada and the Commonwealth Caribbean countries, as well as have negative implications on their socio-political development.

The research was made possible by a Canadian International Development Agency (CIDA) fellowship, administered through the Canadian Bureau for International Education (CBIE). The fellowship provided an

[1] CARICOM is a group of thirteen English-speaking countries (former British colonies), which formed this regional grouping in 1973 for the purpose of enhancing regional trade and economic development. CARICOM countries include Antigua and Barbuda, the Bahamas, Barbados, Belize, Dominica, Grenada, Guyana, Jamaica, Montserrat, St. Kitts and Nevis, St. Lucia, St. Vincent and the Grenadines, and Trinidad and Tobago (See Figure 1, page 9).

opportunity for data to be compiled from both primary and secondary sources. Interviews were conducted with government officials, academics and members of the private sector, social groups and think tanks in Canada, the US and Mexico, including international organizations such as the World Bank and the Interamerican Development Bank (IDB).

Caribbean countries visited for the interviews included were Trinidad, Jamaica, Guyana, Barbados, St. Lucia, Antigua and Grenada. Of these, the latter three are considered lesser-developed countries (LDCs), while the rest are more developed countries (MDCs). Secondary sources included data from the World Bank, CARICOM, the Caribbean Development Bank (CDB), the IDB, the United Nations Economic Commission for Latin America and the Caribbean (ECLAC), newspapers and a number of academic journals. Since this is a new area of research very little data is available, thus limiting the data base upon which this study is based.

The Commonwealth Caribbean is uniquely vulnerable to changes in the international economic environment because of their openness and fragmented nature. These factors have contributed to political and social unrest in many of those countries in the late seventies and were instrumental in motivating the US administration to implement its Caribbean Basin Initiative (CBI).

The US and Canada have had a somewhat different relationship with Caribbean countries. Over the past thirty years the US attempted to "fill the void left by the Europeans, especially the British and to provide support for pro-Western...governments."[2] Current US interest is based on the Caribbean's close geographic proximity and the presence of a sizeable immigrant community which is playing an increasing role in local US politics.[3] Canada's relationship with the Caribbean has for a long period been described as 'special.' This special relationship has been based on historical Commonwealth ties, including trade with eastern Canada. Current Canadian interest in the Caribbean can be described as 'cautious' and is considerably less active than it had been in the past. Since the mid-eighties, Caribbean countries have been recipients of one-way free trade with the United States and Canada through the Caribbean Basin Initiative (CBI) and CARIBCAN, a trading agreement between Canada and the Commonwealth Caribbean. While CBI and CARIBCAN have been less than successful in stimulating the economic growth and investment sought by the region, they are considered to have contributed to the industrial diversification of Caribbean economies.

When the Canada-US Free Trade Agreement (FTA) came into force in January of 1989, it had a minimal effect on existing agreements between the US, Canada and the Caribbean.[4] Less than two years after

---

[2] Center for Strategic and International Studies, U.S.-Caribbean Relations Into the 21st Century, Ed. Georges A. Fauriol, Vol. 11, Report No. 10 (Washington: CSIS Caribbean Research Group, November 15, 1991), p.3.

[3] Ibid.

[4] Conference Board of Canada. "Impact of Canada-US Free Trade on Commonwealth Caribbean countries." A Report Prepared for the Department of External Affairs. October, 1988.

the FTA, Caribbean countries are faced with the formation of a North American free trade agreement which proposes to include Mexico, another developing country. The possible implementation of the NAFTA is one of the most formidable challenges to Caribbean countries in the 1990s. Moreover, the expected economic benefits to the Caribbean countries of including Mexico in a NAFTA have not been clearly assessed.

This study begins by examining the concept of Free Trade with particular reference to the Canada-US FTA, CARICOM and CARIBCAN. The study examines a number of problems with the free trade theory. For example, the impact on free trade of special protection granted to certain industries as a result of political pressure exerted on US and Canadian governments by powerful industrial lobbyists. Such protection is an important element in both the CBI and CARIBCAN. Chapter 1 concludes that there is no such thing as 'free trade', only freer trade.

In Chapter 2, the Enterprise for the Americas Initiative, otherwise known as the 'Bush Proposal,' is examined in detail. This initiative proposes to extend free trade to countries in the Caribbean and Latin American region. The expected social, economic and political benefits of the free trade component of the EAI, as well as the proposed investment and debt relief, investment and debt relief, are controversial from the point-of-view of Commonwealth Caribbean countries. Many of these countries are ill-equipped to cope with competition from more- developed countries in North America and Latin America. The investment component, like that of the CBI, is likely to be minimal. Similarly, the debt component is unlikely to help most Caribbean countries, with the possible exception possibly, of Jamaica and Guyana. Moreover, the debt component could hinder politicians from implementing programs for their constituents while resources intended for these programmes are shifted to the private sector. Such a policy could have implications for the democratic process in the region.

One option available to Caribbean countries, in light of challenges that may result from the Enterprise for the Americas Initiative, is regional integration. In chapter three, it is suggested that regional integration, while no panacea in itself, could help to focus attention on the region and strengthen its bargaining position. However, the prospects of deepening this process is regarded with some pessimism but it is only through regional integration that these countries can adequately meet the challenges.

In order to test the validity of the hypothesis at the functional level, the garment industry, a sector most likely to be affected by a NAFTA, is examined in chapter 4. This sector was chosen because it represents one of the few successful attempts by most Caribbean countries to industrialize. The garment industry is one which is dependent on low wages. Even without free trade, Mexico poses a formidable challenge to the garment industry in the Caribbean. Thus, a NAFTA would increase Mexico's competitive advantage vis-à-vis the Caribbean.

Following the analysis of the garment industry, the results of the study are summarized. The inclusion of Mexico in a NAFTA is likely to increase competition for Caribbean countries, particularly in labour-intensive sectors such as the garment industry. Larger Caribbean countries such as the Dominican Republic and Jamaica, are more likely to suffer from competition from Mexico than the smaller countries.

Freer trade, however, is unlikely to solve the problems of small Caribbean economies. Fragile industries will find it hard to survive competition from more developed economies of North America and Latin America. One-way free trade between North America and the Commonwealth Caribbean resulted in an imbalance on the side of the more developed economies. A similar process may be anticipated if two-way trade is implemented without adequate provision and rationalization of domestic industries. Recent analyses have shown that the process of adjustment to free trade with the US has been hard for Canada, which had a ten-year adjustment period and has the resources to help cushion the blow. One can therefore imagine how much harder the process will be for Caribbean economies in their present state of fragmentation and without the necessary economic resources.

It will be necessary for Caribbean economies, particularly the larger countries, to adjust to the lost jobs as a result of the increased Mexican competition and lack of new investment. It is suggested that one answer would be for the US and Canada to extend similar special trading arrangements to the Caribbean as are being considered for Mexico, particularly because a NAFTA is likely to negate the effectiveness of existing agreements between the US, Canada and Caribbean countries.

A number of innovative approaches to the problems highlighted are required by the Commonwealth Caribbean to meet the challenges of these new trade initiatives. Regional integration emerges as the most viable strategy in light of the challenges that may be posed by a NAFTA and other trading blocs worldwide. If regional integration is to be achieved it will require leadership from those of the political elite who are able to look beyond the immediate economic problems to a more united Caribbean economic bloc.

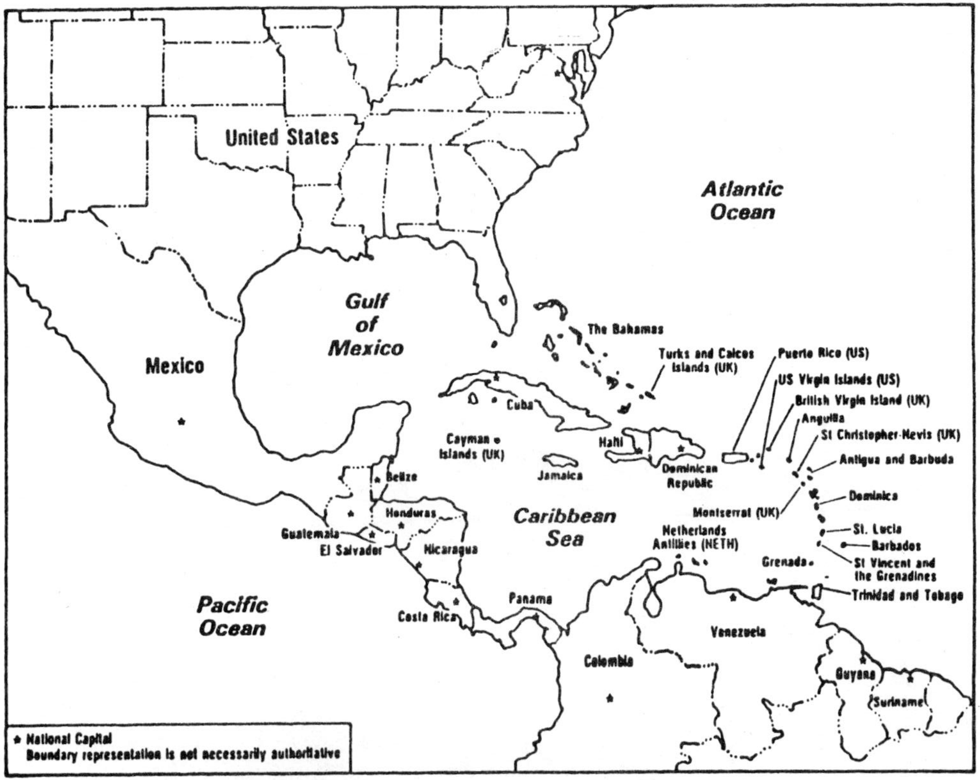

Source: The Atlantic Council of the United States (Washington: OELGESCHIAGER, GUNN & HAIN, 1984) p. XIV.

Chapter 1

Theory and Practice of Free Trade in the Americas: From the Canada-United States FTA to CARIBCAN

Writing in 1983 about the possibility of North American Free trade, with special emphasis on US-Mexico relations, Sidney Weintraub, who specialises in US-Mexican affairs, speculated that the granting of one-way free trade by the US for most products exported by beneficiary countries in the Caribbean and Central America into the United States (under the then proposed Caribbean Basin Initiative (CBI), "could adversely affect some Mexican exports to the United States since they would then face discrimination." (Mexico was not part of the CBI).[1] Weintraub's point is of particular relevance to the subject now being reviewed. For instance, can a similar reverse argument be made by Caribbean countries with regard to the proposed NAFTA?

To the Caribbean Common Market or CARICOM countries this issue is important because these countries enjoy one-way free trade with both the US and Canada and are currently experiencing economic

---

[1] S. Weintraub, "North American Free Trade, With Emphasis on US-Mexico Relations." Paper prepared for the International Studies Association 24th Annual Convention, Mexico City, April 5-9, 1983. p.27.

decline.[2] Indeed, the standard of living in most of those countries was lower in 1990 than in the 1970s.[3] In addition, CARICOM countries face the challenge of a single European market in 1992, an event that could put in jeopardy other preferential arrangements under the European Economic Community (EEC)-sponsored Lomé Convention agreement which favours the former colonies of Community members.

This paper will begin by examining the concept of free trade within the context of the Canada/US agreement. The one-way free trade agreements, The Caribbean Basin Initiative I and II, that exist between the US and the Caribbean will be assessed. CARIBCAN, the Canadian trade agreement with the region, will also be examined in relation to the North American Free Trade Agreement.

The issue of free trade between Canada and the US has been a recurrent theme in Canada-US relations over a number of years. It was once dubbed the "issue that won't die." Since the Reciprocity Treaty between 1854 and 1866, a failed attempt to reestablish reciprocity in 1874 and the Canadian elections in 1878, 1891 and 1911, all of which focused on the issue, free trade has been a recurrent theme in Canadian politics.[4]

---

[2] CARICOM countries include Antigua and Barbuda, the Bahamas, Barbados, Belize, Dominica, Grenada, Guyana, Jamaica, Montserrat, St. Kitts and Nevis, St. Lucia, St. Vincent and the Grenadines, and Trinidad and Tobago.

[3] Assessment based on World Bank Report, The Caribbean Common Market: Trade Policies and Regional Integration in the 1990s, (Washington: December 21, 1990), p.12.

[4] Canada, Backgrounder "Canada-US Free Trade Agreement, (Ottawa: Library of Parliament, January 27, 1988),p.2.

A Free Trade agreement involves the elimination of tariff and non-tariff barriers to trade between signatory countries, with each maintaining its respective tariff schedules with non-member nations. The US - Canada FTA, which came into effect on January 1st, 1989, represents the loosest form of economic integration, involving only the removal of mutual trade barriers.[5] The Canada/US FTA is designed to eliminate virtually all tariffs between the two countries within ten years. One of the first proponents of the idea of free trade was Adam Smith. He saw it as, among other things, a way of promoting efficiency, both because it fostered competition and because it provided opportunities to specialise and gain economies of scale via the concept of 'absolute advantage'. Smith held that trade allows countries to produce what they produce best and to buy other products from other countries.[6] What Smith's formula did not address was what would happen if one country was less efficient than a number of countries in just about everything. Would this mean that the country in question would have to give up trading altogether? [7]

In response to this Smithian weakness, David Ricardo, the economist, writing some 40 years later, formulated the principle of 'comparative advantage.' In his Principles of Political Economy and Taxation (1817), Ricardo provided the first "scientific" demonstration that international trade is mutually beneficial. His law of comparative advantage

---

[5] Backgrounder:p. 2.

[6] The Economist, "World Trade: Jousting for Advantage",(London: September 22, 1990) Vol. 316, No. 7673, p.12.

[7] Ibid.: p. 12.

or cost provided a new basis for liberal trade theory and is used as the fundamental rationale for free trade.[8]

Ricardo recognized that "the flow of trade among countries is determined by the relative (not absolute) costs of the goods, produced." Although a nation may have an absolute advantage over others in the production of every good, it will tend to specialize in those commodities whose costs are comparatively lowest, leaving the production of other commodities to other countries, which, in theory, would encourage countries to gain via exchange.

The classical theory of trade, propounded by Ricardo, John Stuart Mill and other classical Liberals, was based on a number of assumptions. It assumed that the factors of production, such as capital and labour, were mobile domestically but immobile internationally. The theory of comparative advantage was regarded as static, a gift of nature which could not be transferred from one country to another. The theory was also based on the labour theory of value, which held that the amount and efficiency of labour input is the main determinant of the cost of production. Furthermore, the law of comparative advantage was based on the model of two countries.[9]

These assumptions have all been questioned. First, the classical model omitted the cost of transportation. This has subsequently been added by neo classical writers, making the theory more realistic.

---

[8] Robert Gilpin, The Political Economy of International Relations (Princeton: Princeton Univ. Press, 1987), p. 173.

[9] Gilpin: p. 175.

Second, modified trade theory has assumed greater mobility of the factors of production among countries. Third, the importance of increasing returns to scale have also been added to explain contemporary trade. Furthermore, the dynamic nature of comparative advantage, for instance, the mobility of capital, has been recognised. Contemporary trade theory combines mathematical techniques and statistical data. Determination of the cost of production now includes factors other than labour itself. Contemporary theorists now speak of "human capital," while the cost concept incorporates "opportunity cost."[10]

Neoclassical economics is now called the Heckscher-Ohlin theory (H-O), model of International trade. This version of the comparative cost doctrine provides a measure of comparative advantage that does not depend on the existence of perfect competition and initial equilibrium.[11]

The H-O model represents the standard liberal position in the 1990s. Its essential position is that "a nation's comparative advantage is determined by the relative abundance and most profitable combination of its several factors of production, such as capital, labour, resources, management, and technology."[12] The recognition of these factors make modern trade theory more comprehensive and dynamic than its classical counterpart. Nevertheless, it has become increasingly recognised that the

---

[10] Gilpin: p. 176.

[11] See Ramesh Ramsaran, The Commonwealth Caribbean in the World Economy,(Warwick: Warwick Univ. Press Caribbeean Studies, 1989), Note 12, p.163.

[12] Gilpin: p. 176.

complexity of international trade and the fact that countries do not have equal access to the same production technology make it difficult to explain trade patterns by one theory or model. For instance, industralised countries are more sophisticated technologically and this gives them easy access to foreign markets in the early stages of manufacture. One of the most vocal critics of the neo-classical model, Mark Anderson, an international economist for the American AFL-CIO, holds that "all the theories of classical economics have been rendered irrelevant by the globalization of capital and the monopoly nature of international business." Anderson argues that "When capital can move anywhere in the world at any time, you can't talk about comparative advantage any more. What comparative advantage does a Mexican worker have except his poverty?"[13] Other arguments point to the size of the domestic market. Where economies of scale exist, lower costs will encourage products to enter foreign markets easier. This does not mean that small countries cannot compete. Access to mobile capital and foreign markets has enabled a number of small countries, such as Korea, to compete in the world economy.

One of the most obvious omissions in the free trade theory is the important role of politics, which has always made the goal of free trade a myth rather than a reality. The politics of trade is most evident in the implementation of non-tariff barriers, and subjective rules of origin. Because "free trade" has never been practiced in the real world, it is hard to judge

[13] Francis Russell, "Free Trade Initiative Poses Threat to Workers Jobs," Winnipeg Free Press, (Winnipeg: January 26, 1991), p.1.

whether it would be a success. Indeed, a recent analysis of free trade areas, undertaken by the Institute for International Economics, has concluded that there is no such thing as 'free trade' only 'freer trade.'[14] Schott holds that multilateral trade, as practiced through membership in the General Agreement on Tariffs and Trade (GATT), is less likely to divert trade and is more likely to provide gains and dispute settlement mechanisms for weaker trading nations.[15] A principal reason for seeking free trade agreements is that it is generally harder to get agreement on the part of many countries. This is evident in the current GATT negotiations, otherwise referred to as the Uruguay Round, which has been deadlocked over the question of agricultural subsidies, among other items.

Although free trade between Canada and the US has been on the Canadian political burner for a number of years, there were a number of circumstances which contributed to the signing of the Canada/US FTA in the 1980s. First, a series of bilateral agreements had liberalized trade over a number of years, culminating in the agreement. Second, the experience of the Auto Pact, negotiated in 1965, had demonstrated to both countries the feasibility of free trade in at least one sector. Third, there was a growing recognition in both countries that the world was becoming one market and that a greater degree of competitiveness was required, both

---

[14] Jeffrey J. Schott, More Free Trade Areas? (Washington: Institute for International Economics, May 1989), No. 27, p.24.

[15] Schott: p. 25.

domestically and internationally.[16] A fourth factor was Canada's need for more secure access to the US market. Existing access appeared to be threatened by growing protectionist sentiment in the US market. An additional factor was the personal and political relationship that had built up between Prime Minister Brian Mulroney and President Ronald Reagan, based on a certain similarity of world view. Mulroney had committed Canada to a policy of "excellent relations with our neighbours to the South" during the federal elections in l985. The highlights of the Agreement are as follows: All tariffs between Canada and the US are to be removed within a period of ten years, including non-tariff barriers. The Agreement which includes services, as well as goods and investment between the two countries, has been liberalized, in recognition of the interconnectedness of trade and investment. The inclusion of both services and investment adds a distinctive element to the agreement. Another important feature is its dispute-solving mechanism. In recognition of the potential obstacles to free trade, a bi-national dispute settlement mechanism has been set up to settle disputes, which are recognised to be generally of a political nature.[17] The FTA also facilitates business travel between the two countries, thus serving to free up human capital.[18]

Although free trade has been associated with the Liberal party, the Progressive Conservative (PC) government has made the FTA an

---

[16] Royal Bank of Canada, Econoscope, "Free Trade Agreement: One-Year Retrospective," (Montreal: Jan. 18, 1990), Vol. 13, No 11-12, p.3.

[17] Econoscope: p. 3.

[18] Ibid.

important part of its economic development strategy. Debates leading up to the l985 federal election saw the free trade side, or continentalists, argue that economic gains would flow from free trade for the following reasons: Lower prices for imports would increase consumers' real disposable income and decrease the cost inputs from firms. The anticipated shift in production towards those goods produced at a relatively lower cost, would allow Canadian industry to exploit its comparative advantage more fully. Canada's vast resources have always been considered a comparative advantage, but the argument put forward by free trade proponants is that increased imports would enhance competition, promote efficiency and lower the price of domestically-produced goods.

Canadian manufacturing plants would then specialize and expand to meet increased US demand, thus exploiting economies of scale; and, with prices determined abroad, existing Canadian exporters would benefit from the duty formerly paid to the US treasury.[19]

On the other hand, many of the critics of free trade such as the two opposition parties and organised labour in Canada, believe that the removal of Canadian tariffs would result in massive job dislocation and high transition costs. They argue that, if Canadian manufacturing could not compete with the US sector, Canadian manufacturing production and jobs would eventually be replaced by production and employment in the US; elimination of Canadian tariffs would permit US-owned companies to pull up stakes and shift production south of the border where they would supply the entire North American market. This has indeed occurred to some

[19] Backgrounder: p. 3.

extent since free trade was implemented. It has also been argued that employment gains would be made in the resource-based industries at the cost of manufacturing jobs, resulting in Canadians increasingly becoming "hewers of wood and drawers of water."[20]

These critics have emphasized the transition costs of free trade, particularly in sectors seen as most vulnerable to US competition. Canadian industry could be modernised, more effectively and humanely they suggest, by an industrial strategy that selectively rewarded the winners and phased out the losers, instead of through a "cold shower" provided by free trade.[21]

While economic forecasts predict long-term economic gains for Canada ranging between 3% and 8% of Canadian GNP,[22] the major unresolved question regarding free trade in the Canada-US context lies outside the economic sphere. Most critics of free trade argue that free trade would involve a loss of Canadian sovereignty, as negotiators would be required to sacrifice domestic social policies, including those dealing with Canadian culture and regional development. In addition, critics charge that a free trade agreement would represent an irreversible step on a road leading to Canada's complete economic and political integration with the US. As evidence, critics of free trade point to the annexation of Hawaii by

---

[20] Backgrounder: p. 4.

[21] Ibid.

[22] Royal Commission on the Economic Union and Development Prospects for Canada (Macdonald Commission), Final Report (Ottawa: Supply and Services, 1985), Vol. 1, pp. 213-275.

the US after free trade between the two countries was established. Supporters, however, argue that countries like Holland or Belgium have not suffered an undue loss of sovereignty after joining the EEC.[23]

Since all agreements require certain concessions, the Canada -US FTA is likely to be judged on the basis of a cost benefit analysis, in other words, whether its benefits outweigh its costs, including its dispute resolution mechanism, while the issue of sovereignty is likely to rest on the degree of restrictions the agreement places on the actions of future governments.[24]

Free trade negotiations between the US and Mexico, less than two years after the signing of the Canada/US FTA, seems to have taken the Canadian government by surprise. This was apparent when Prime Minister Brian Mulroney addressed the heads of government of the Commonwealth Caribbean in Barbados in March, 1990.[25] Canada's response was to request that it be included in the US-Mexico negotiations, on a trilateral basis, in order to preclude any watering down of the Canada-US FTA, and to ensure Canada's equal access to the Mexican economy. Canada's concerns were supported by Jeffrey J. Schott of the Institute for International Economics "Each new US agreement would undercut the value of concessions obtained by partner countries in previous FTAs, because

---

[23] Backgrounder: p. 5.

[24] Ibid.: p. 6.

[25] Discussion with Mr. Lester Bird, former Deputy Prime Minister of Antigua, April 13, 1991; interview with the Rt. Hon. John Compton, Prime Minister, St. Lucia, April 7, 1991.

the preferences in the US market would be shared, and thus diluted, by the new FTA partners."[26] On the other hand, critics of the government argue that Canada runs the risk of having the FTA opened up once again with possible gains for the US. This, they say, would be the price of allowing the Americans to set the political agenda.[27]

Free trade is viewed by the Americans as an issue with potential impact on other bilateral concerns with Mexico. Other foreign policy objectives, apart from trade and investment, have to do with Mexico's ability to make its international debt payments. It is estimated that some $30 billion is currently owed to US financial institutions. Other concerns are the control of illegal emigration from Mexico to the US, the flow of documented workers and the preventing of the abuse of Mexican workers who cross the US -Mexican border; and a reduction in the flow of illegal narcotics from Mexico to the US by engaging in bilateral efforts to curb both supply and demand.[28] Not least of all, the US would gain access to cheap labour, and a market for its products, expand its financial service sector and help to underwrite economic and political reform in Mexico.[29]

The coincidence of US-Mexico free trade talks and the current round of GATT negotiations has fueled speculation about US motives. One

---

[26] Schott: p. 25.

[27] Backgrounder: p. 6.

[28] US Congress, Regional Brief "US-Mexico Relations" (Washington: May 1989), pp.1-4.

[29] Les Whittington and Anne McIlroy, "The Flipside of Boom" in The Ottawa Citizen (Ottawa: May 5, 1991) p.E7.

school of thought holds that the US purposely encouraged free trade talks with Mexico as a card up its sleeve to help it make headway in its GATT negotiations. Another view is that a free trade zone in the Americas will provide secure markets for the United States and others in the region, in light of the current trend which appears to be favouring trading blocs, such as the European Economic Community and similar formations in Asia. It is well known that the US Administration is dissatisfied with the role played by GATT in the past few years.

A NAFTA would create a North American market of some 360 million people. Mexico's population is over 8O million and the country has an abundance of inexpensive labour, roughly one tenth the cost of that in the US. The combined economy of all three countries would approximate $6 trillion a year. This would compare with a European Common Market in 1992 of 336 million people and an economy of about $4.4 trillion a year.[30]

Mexico has made a significant effort to liberalise its economy over the past few years and is attracting considerable attention from industry. While the debt crisis is considered critical in influencing the present Mexican government to liberalize its economy, there are other factors at work. The present government of President Carlos Salinas de Gortari, a Harvard-educated economist, is banking on Mexico's relative "comparative advantage," cheap labour, and the country's proximity to the US to attract much-needed employment and foreign investment. Unemployment in Mexico is estimated to be around 40 percent and the

[30] Ibid.: p. E7.

country needs to improve infrastructure, especially communications, in order to attract more investment.[31] President Salinas, unlike previous nationalist governments of Mexico, is betting on the gains from free trade to give his country much-needed economic growth. A number of state-run industries have been privatised. Companies such as Canada's Spar Aerospace Ltd., which sells communications systems, have promoted the benefits of doing business in Mexico. Other Canadian companies appear equally impressed. "The opportunities are boundless," says Doug Clark, general manager of Northern Telecom's Mexican operations.[32]

Mexico would certainly benefit from a NAFTA, but would the Commonwealth Caribbean, which is not party to the agreement? In order to evaluate the possible impact of a NAFTA on the Commonwealth Caribbean, it is necessary to review the existing trading agreements between the US, Canada and the Caribbean. It is important to point out, however, that, since talks between the United States, Mexico and Canada are far from completion, this study is limited in its scope to identifying those sectors that are likely to be most sensitive from the Caribbean perspective. Since 1983 the United States (US) has promoted its Caribbean Basin Initiative, better known as the CBI, as a plan to revitalise the failing economies of the English-speaking countries of the Caribbean and certain countries of Central America. The Plan, which was introduced in the US legislature in 1983 as the Caribbean Basin Economic Recovery Act

[31] Ibid.

[32] Christian Allard, "Mexico for Sale: Gringos Welcome" in Canadian Business (Toronto: November 1990), p.74.

(CBERA), offered the region one-way free trade to the US market. Except for a certain number of exemptions, any items of Caribbean Basin products can enter the US duty-free. But the items must be produced, grown, or manufactured in a beneficiary country and meet "rules-of-origin" requirements. For instance, they must be imported directly from a beneficiary; at least 35 percent of the value of the item must be added in one or more beneficiaries; and the product must be substantially transformed in one or more of the beneficiaries.[33] In addition to the duty-free treatment, the CBI offers tax incentives to US companies who attend conventions in the region. This provision only applies, however, if the beneficiary country enters into an agreement with the US agreeing to an exchange of tax information.[34]

The CBI was seen by many as the United States' reaction to the rise of socialist regimes in the region in the late 1970s.[35] Only non-socialist states that agreed to comply with certain preconditions were considered eligible CBI countries. Thus, the plan excluded Cuba, Nicaragua and initially Grenada and Guyana. Furthermore, the plan sought to redefine the Caribbean by including a number of Central American countries into a new grouping known as the Caribbean Basin. Nevertheless, since its inception, the CBI, which was well-promoted by the

---

33 33 The World Bank, The Caribbean: Export Preferences and Performance, (Washington: December, 1988), p. 68.

34 Ibid.

35 Jennifer Hosten-Craig, "The CBI: An Analysis and a Critique" (Ottawa: Carleton Univ. Honours Thesis, 1989).

Reagan administration, managed to create a great deal of expectation on the part of member countries.

The economic impact of the CBI in the region has been described as generally disappointing, since most of the benefits originally anticipated have not born fruit. Certain modest gains, however, have been realized by the Region in exports of certain non-traditional Caribbean goods such as electrical equipment, fruit, flowers and winter vegetables.[36]

Although the trading performance of member states varied between l983 and 1989, US exports to the region increased while those from the Caribbean declined. In part, the decline was due to decreases in the imports of oil from Trinidad and Tobago and of sugar and bauxite from the region in general.[37]

The initial CBI fell short in several ways. First of all, it excluded any specific provisions to stimulate investment, or technical assistance to develop the economic infrastructure. Secondly, it excluded products for which the region has a demonstrated capability and which are labour-intensive, such as textiles and garments, leather goods and petroleum products.[38] Thirdly, CBI I did not address the issue of non-tariff barriers. Caribbean producers report enormous difficulties in penetrating

---

[36] CARICOM document, Regional Response to the Bush Proposal- "Enterprise for the Americas," April, 1991, p. 1.

[37] Ibid.

[38] Ibid.

the US market because of quotas, labelling requirements, standards and various administrative and legislative activities, all of which have served to limit trade.[39]

In response to the criticism levied against CBI 1, the Reagan administration announced a new scheme (not part of the CBI) in February 1986 to permit higher levels for garment exports from the Caribbean. The scheme, referred to as "super 807" or guaranteed access level (GAL)," [40] allows garments made from cloth woven and cut in the US to enjoy guaranteed minimum access levels, although not on a completely duty-free basis. Duty is charged only on the labour- or value-added component. To date, Haiti, the Dominican Republic, Jamaica and Trinidad and Tobago have signed the appropriate bilateral agreements. President Reagan also gave support in 1985 to a proposal made by the government of Puerto Rico to use government development funds for investment under the CBI. The plan, known as the 936, requires the creation of twin plant manufacturing, by which Caribbean countries are to provide low-cost labour for items manufactured in the US and Puerto Rico.[41]

Although the Reagan administration attempted to improve the benefits of trade and investment by legislation, referred to as CBI II, it too has been thwarted by strong protectionist sentiments on the part of the US Congress and the efforts of special interest lobbies. While several

---

[39] Ibid.

[40] World Bank, The Caribbean: Export Preferences and Performance, (Washington: December, 1988) p. 68.

[41] Ramsaran, p. 141.

measures were suggested to improve the trading regime, only one important area of improvement has been made. The life of CBI 11 has been extended for an indefinite period, rather than the 12-year maximum originally allowed under CBI 1. This change will eliminate some of the uncertainty that a fixed number of years created.[42]

The difficulties encountered by CARICOM countries, despite being granted one-way duty-free trade with the world's richest country, highlights some of the problems of conventional economic theory. Conventional theory holds that, when small countries, such as those in the Caribbean, and a very large country such as the United States, integrate their economies, the small country stands to gain "the preponderance of the gains from trade."[43] Although the US and Caribbean Basin countries do not meet all the assumptions of the contemporary model, it is nevertheless worthy of note that the country that has benefitted the most (by an average of 18 percent in 1987, over the 1983 average) is not any of the small countries but rather the United States. [44]

CBI is underutilized for a number of reasons. Its limitations, exacerbated by strong US producers' lobbies, are well documented. Discussions with involved parties in most of the islands pointed to the difficulty incurred in exporting to the US, particularly non-traditional

---

[42] CARICOM, April, 1991: p. 2.

[43] Winston H. Griffith," CARICOM Countries and the Caribbean Basin Initiative" in Latin American Perspectives Issue 64, Vol.17 No. 1 Winter 1990, pp.33-54, p.34.

[44] Business America, (Washington: April 25, 1988), pp. 42-43.

products. This was seen to be particularly difficult for small individual exporters. The cost of promotion in order to break into the US market was one major obstacle since it is not easy for such costs to be spread over small volumes. It has been suggested that niche markets, or markets specific to a particular product, should be identified by area producers.[45] While CBI exclusions have not helped the trade performance of CARICOM, at least one analyst, Winston H. Griffith, points to a number of more basic problems facing Caribbean economies. Among these are the lack of an entrepreneural class and the need for greater incentives on the part of CARICOM countries to increase regional industrial appeal. Griffith suggests the following measures: restructuring the regional economies through decentralisation measures, more attention to technological development and improving regional infrastructure. An additional problem, according to Griffith, is the free-trade policies being followed by many regional governments under the CBI, which, according to Griffith, are "making it more difficult to diversify the region's agricultural base" because the relatively small food sector is being undermined.[46] Griffith has pointed to the work of Gerald M. Meier to substantiate his argument that free trade between significantly different economies "may constitute formidable obstacles to ... (the less developed) achieving self-sustaining growth."[47] Thus, Griffith concludes that the free-trade approach, encouraged by the

[45] Interviews with Adrian Ojay of the St. Lucia Chamber of Commerce, April 2, 1991, and JAMPRO representative, Jamaica, April, 1991.

[46] Griffith: pp. 35-49.

[47] Griffith: pp. 112-118.

US under the CBI, might benefit some US industries but is unlikely to stimulate industry in CARICOM countries at their present level of development.[48] Lack of interest by US authorities in CBI II has led regional analysts to believe that the US is no longer willing to continue its donor/beneficiary relationship with the region. This unwillingness is indicated by the two-way free trade proposals suggested in the latest American Initiative for the region, the Enterprise for the Americas Initiative (EAI). This new initiative takes on added importance in light of a NAFTA and will be discussed in chapter two.

Assessment of the impact of a NAFTA and of its likely extension in the form of the EAI to include areas such as the Caribbean also requires an evaluation of the current trading agreement that exists between Canada and the CARICOM countries.

When CARIBCAN was implemented in 1986, it represented yet another step in strengthening what most people in the CARICOM countries consider a "special relationship" between Canada and the former British colonies of the region.[49] Canadian-Caribbean trading relations go back as far as the early eighteenth century to the colonial history of the two areas, when Atlantic Canada traded fish and timber for rum, sugar and molasses with the West Indies.[50] Indeed, it was disappointment over the

---

[48] Ibid.: p. 49.

[49] See Introduction for explanation of the CBI and CARIBCAN.

[50] See Jennifer Hosten-Craig, CARIBCAN: An Analysis and Alternative Strategies (Ottawa: Carleton Univ. unpublished paper, 1989), p.9.

CBI which led Caribbean leaders to turn to Canada for improved access to its market.[51]

However, when CARIBCAN was signed in 1986, it was seen as Canada's version of the CBI,[52] particularly because the one-way free trade agreement, which was extended to eighteen English-speaking countries in the Caribbean (13 of them being members of CARICOM) sought to exclude many of the same items that had been excluded under the CBI. These included textiles and clothing, footwear, leather garments, lubrication oils and methanol.[53] In addition, like the CBI, it lacked an investment component, thought by many in the region to be necessary, although the federal government did enable its Trade Facilitation Office (TFO) to provide seminars on trade, funding for trade fairs, publication of marketing information for exporters and the like.[54] CARIBCAN's stated goal was to "facilitate trade, development assistance and industrial cooperation with Commonwealth Caribbean countries."[55]

---

[51] Ibid: p. 3.

[52] See Catherine Hyett, "CARIBCAN: Canada's Response to the Caribbean Basin Initiative" (Kingston: Queens Univ., 1989); unpublished paper.

[53] Hosten-Craig, 1990: 5.

[54] Ibid.: p. 8.

[55] Government of Canada, News Release, March 19, 1990 p.1.

Prior to CARIBCAN, the Caribbean was already a recipient of the General Preferential Tariff (GPT) and the British Preferential Tariff (BPT) for which certain products from the Caribbean states were eligible.[56]

There are some important differences, however, between the CBI and CARIBCAN. First of all, CARIBCAN was not seen to have been ideologically motivated. It did not seek to exclude socialist countries in the region but appeared instead to focus on the English-speaking countries with which it had established trading relations. Secondly, its low-key approach did not excite any undue or unrealistic expectations, as was the case with the CBI. There are still a number of traders in the region with little knowledge of the potential trading opportunities available under CARIBCAN.[57]

CARIBCAN provides for preferential duty-free access to the Canadian market for roughly 98 percent of the goods produced by Commonwealth Caribbean countries till 1998. At that time the program will be reevaluated.[58]

Another provision of CARIBCAN is that a minimum of 50 percent of ex-factory price of goods must originate in any of the beneficiary countries or in Canada. The ex-factory price includes the cost of

---

[56] Ramsaran: p. 28.

[57] Hosten-Craig paper, (1990) and interviews in the region, February, March and April, 1991.

[58] Stanley Reid, Significance/Relevance of the Canada-US Free Trade Agreement With Particular Reference to the Caribbean: Some Perspectives, (Barbados: Export Promotion Corporation Special Symposium, April 3-5, 1990), p. 116.

production, packaging and profits, and excise duties must still be paid on liquors, tobacco, cigarettes, jewellery and gasoline.[59]

CARIBCAN, like the CBI, has had little success in reversing the trend towards growing regional trade deficits. Indeed, Canada's trade surplus with the Commonwealth Caribbean declined from $86 million in 1981 to $28 million in 1985. In 1988, Canadian trade had climbed to $84 million, close to its 1986 level. This is a similar trend to that noticed in the US following the CBI's creation. Between 1985 and 1988, the value of Canada's total imports from CARIBCAN economies increased only slightly by 3 per cent, from $263 million to $270 million. By contrast, Canadian exports to the Anglophone Caribbean grew by 22 percent or $63 million, from $291 million in 1985 to $354 million in 1988.[60]

In response to the expressed disillusionment by Caribbean leaders concerning the CARIBCAN exclusions, certain changes have been announced by the Canadian government. On March 19, 1990, Prime Minister Brian Mulroney announced that the list of items from countries covered by CARIBCAN qualifying for duty-free access into Canada had been extended to include leather luggage and certain vegetable fibre products. In addition, the Prime Minister noted that changes had been made to Canadian regulations permitting the bottling in Canada of Commonwealth Caribbean rum with only a minimal blending requirement. It was also announced that the government of Canada would open a

---

[59] Reid: p. 117.

[60] Canada, Statistics Canada, "Trade of Canada, Imports by Country, 1981-1988, Table 2.

Business Cooperation office in Ottawa to promote long-term business linkages throughout the region for the benefit of Canadian and Caribbean interests. Last, but by no means least, was the announcement by Canada's Prime Minister that the region's bilateral debts would be forgiven.[61]

CARIBCAN, like the CBI, is underutilized, possibly because of inadequate knowledge of the Canadian market and poor promotion of the free trade facility. Conversations with various members of the private sector revealed that they had little knowledge of the initiative.[62] Joint Canadian/Caribbean promotion is needed. In practical terms, little is known of the trade facilitation office in Ottawa, despite its establishment to promote Canadian investment and trade. It was generally felt that CARIBCAN could have an increased impact if it increased its focus on training and joint ventures and implemented a similar program such as the super 807, which facilitate the export of garments to the American market. This will become evident in the analysis of the garment industry in chapter 2. While all of these suggestions would make a difference, the overriding problem facing regional exports to the Canadian market is the lack of regular, affordable transportation. Most shipments destined for Canada are shipped via Miami or New York.[63]

---

[61] News Release by the Government of Canada, March 19, 1990, p.1.

[62] Bonnie Zephrin, of Viking Traders, Castries, St. Lucia, April, 1991; Mr. Gary Voss, President of the Manufacturers Assoc. Port-of-Spain, Trinidad, March 20, 1991; Mr. Richard Thomas, President of Electro Assembly (Antigua), Ltd. April, 1991.

[63] Discussion with Michael Miners, President of the Grenada Chamber of Commerce, March, 1991 and Bonnie Zephrin, Viking Traders, St. Lucia,

This brief enquiry has shown that one-way free trade, in the form of the CBI and CARIBCAN, has not resulted in increasing, in any significant way, trade exports from the Commonwealth Caribbean to North America. Growth of trade with the region has ironically occurred in the opposite direction. Although the picture might be significantly improved without present exclusions and non-tariff barriers, it is still worth noting that, CARICOM countries have not maximized the opportunities of one-way trade provided by both the CBI or CARIBCAN. One reason is that Caribbean countries have lacked the capital to mount effective marketing programmes in North America to promote their products. One of the effects of the Canada-US FTA was to put Caribbean fruit and vegetable producers in direct competition with their counterparts in the Southern US and a free trade with Mexico would likely increase the competition in those products, as well as in other sectors.[64]

In the next chapter the full implication of a NAFTA and its extension in the form of the Enterprise for the Americas Initiative (EAI) will be explored in relation to the Commonwealth Caribbean.

April, 1991.

[64] See Conference Board of Canada Report, "Impact of Canada-United States Free Trade on Commonwealth Caribbean Countries,"_(Ottawa), October 1988, p. 6.

Chapter 2

The Enterprise for the Americas Initiative: Its Application to the Commonwealth Caribbean

The Caribbean is caught in a world economic vice.[1]

On June 27, 1990, President George Bush announced the formation of a programme by the US administration which has come to be called the Enterprise for the Americas Initiative (EAI). Like the CBI, the EAI has been touted by many as an answer to the economic stagnation which faces a majority of Caribbean and Latin American countries. But what are the political and social implications of the Bush plan? The argument proposed here is that the plan offers few new perspectives on the solution to the economic problems of the Commonwealth Caribbean. Furthermore, like previous US initiatives, it is designed to impose a US agenda which could have negative socio-political consequences in the region.

The stated purpose of the EAI is to address the debt and investment problems of the region.[2] High levels of accumulated debt and declining investment have curtailed the region's growth potential. This is

---

[1] Hugh Marshall, former Minister of Trade, Antigua.

[2] Minutes of meeting between CARICOM Representatives and Dr. David Mulford, Under Secretary in the US Treasury, Dec 18, 1990, p.1.

particularly true of Latin American countries. Indeed, austerity measures imposed by those countries to address the debt crisis had several effects, one of which was the decline of US exports to that part of the region by $8 billion between 1981 and 1987.[3] While the debt crisis has affected some Caribbean countries more than others, it also remains an obstacle to the attainment of sustained development for them. Concomitantly, the level of foreign investment in most territories has not been sufficient to make-up for the shortage in domestic capital.

While economic problems plague most Commonwealth Caribbean countries, some have prospered in spite of the obstacles. Indeed, in comparison with some developing areas, the Caribbean performance has been better than some and recovery, particularly in the smaller or less-developed countries (LDCs), has in some cases been significant.[4]

Although present circumstances do not allow for complacency, it is the great uncertainty produced by changes to the world economy which presents the English-speaking countries of the region with the greatest challenges to their future development. The possible emergence of European, Asian and American trade blocs, the early negotiation of a US-Mexican-Canadian free trade zone and now President Bush's proposal for a hemisphere-wide free trade zone under the aegis of

---

[3] See Peter Field paper, Trading Ideas: An Integrated, Long Term US Strategy for Latin America, US Dept. of Commerce, 1989, p.15.

[4] Caribbean Development to the Year 2000: Challenges, Prospects and Policies, otherwise known as the Bourne Report, June 1988 p. xvii.

his EAI all have the effect of forcing small Caribbean countries to accept a regime that puts them on a level playing field with larger and more developed neighbouring countries. Added to this is the prognosis, arrived at by the Bourne Report on Caribbean Development to the Year 2000, that "for all Caribbean Community countries (CARICOM), unemployment and falling standards of living are the major problems for the remainder of this century."[5] It is against this background that the EAI will be analysed.

This chapter will outline the main components of the EAI, followed by an analysis of the plan. The possible social and political effects of the EAI will then be examined, supported by a selection of the views and opinions of leading Caribbean personalities.

The Initiative outlines three main "pillars": trade, investment and debt relief which is tied to an environment fund.[6] These components are best remembered by the acronym, TIED (Trade, Investment, Environment and Debt).

The trade component of the EAI proposes the creation of a hemispheric-wide free trade zone, stretching from the northern Yukon to the southern Yucatan. The Canada/US FTA was the first of what is expected to be a series of free trade agreements with the US. A US/Mexico/Canada agreement would be the second of such agreements. Negotiations towards this end began in June, 1991. President Bush has held out the hope that other countries in the Caribbean and Latin America may also be included following the Mexico negotiations.

---

[5] See Bourne Report.

[6] See President Bush's EAI speech, June 27, 1990.

The investment component has two thrusts. As the first, the US would work with the Inter-American Development Bank (IDB) to create a new policy-based lending programme to promote the reform of investment regimes. The programme would provide technical and financial support for privatization efforts and the liberalization of investment regimes. The second part would involve the creation of a five-year multilateral investment fund within the IDB, to advance comprehensive investment reforms. This fund would provide grants of up to $300 million US annually over five years to be funded jointly by the US, the European Economic Community (EEC) and Japan.[7]

The third component is designed to relieve the debt burden of the region by a programme which will refinance and write-off certain regional loans. The three components will be linked to compliance with reform programmes of the IDB, the International Monetary Fund (IMF) or the World Bank. In addition, funds are to be set aside for the preservation of the environment.[8]

Although the EAI is still in its formative stage,[9] some preliminary analysis will be attempted. Indeed, this is possible because CARICOM countries, as well as a number of regional think-tanks, have already undertaken studies on the subject.

---

[7] Roger B. Porter, "The Enterprise for the Americas Initiative: A New Approach to Economic Growth" in Journal of International Studies and World Affairs, Winter 1990, Vol. 32, No. 4, pp. 2-11.

[8] CARICOM document, April, 1991 p.3.

[9] Conversation with officials from the US department of Commerce, Mr. Peter Field. February, 1991, Washington.

The trade component of the EAI is somewhat ambiguous on the issue of whether it favours multilateral or bilateral trade relations. For instance, the Bush statement appears to give priority to groups of countries which are already organised (such as CARICOM) for the purpose of promoting trade: "any interested nation in the region, particularly with groups of countries that have associated for the purpose of trade liberalization."[10] Consequently, Jamaica, often the first CARICOM country to act (Jamaica was a principal mover behind the scenes in both the CBI and CARIBCAN initiatives), was once again the first to express an interest in negotiating a bilateral-framework agreement with the US. However, Jamaica's government has subsequently abandoned its bilateral request in favour of a multilateral approach, following a preliminary agreement by other CARICOM countries to proceed along those lines. Jamaica's decision has ended much speculation that it was willing to abandon its CARICOM partners in order to sign a bilateral framework agreement with the US.

The principal goal of either a bilateral or multilateral agreement is to indicate the interest of applicant countries in the proposal, as stipulated by the Bush statement, and to put countries in line for benefits associated with the Initiative. Mexico signed a bilateral framework agreement committing it to liberalising measures prior to formal free-trade negotiations with the US.

The multilateral/bilateral question could have important implications for CARICOM countries. Article 68 of the Annex to the

[10] See Bush Statement on EAI, June 27, 1990 Congressional Quarterly, Washington, p.2.

CARICOM treaty specifies that, while member states are not precluded from participating in other arrangements, such participation may only be "to the extent that those arrangements are not incompatible with the obligations of member states under this Annex."[11] Article 68 was specifically designed to preclude the possibility of the establishment of different trade arrangements by member states. Similar reasoning was behind the transformation of Commonwealth Caribbean states from CARIFTA to a Common Market (CARICOM) in order to present a united front in negotiations with the European Economic Community.[12]

Despite US rhetoric about free trade, Caribbean countries remember the practical example of CBI I and II. Many analysts in the region feel that, just as protectionist lobbies and vested interests were successful in whittling down the benefits of both CBI I and II, so will US self-interest work against the interests of Caribbean and Latin American countries, thereby minimizing EAI benefits, whenever their views diverge from those of the US.[13] The risk of special interests undermining proposals of the EAI are real since organised labour, both in Canada and the US, have declared their collective opposition to a NAFTA and would likely oppose its extension in the form of the EAI.

Would the benefits of two-way trade for CARICOM countries outweigh the risks of reciprocal trade? CARICOM countries currently enjoy

[11] See CARICOM Treaty Annex, Article 68.

[12] See CARICOM Document USA-CARICOM Economic Relations 11 December, 1990 p.7.

[13] Ibid.

free trade on a non-reciprocal basis into the US and Canadian markets for a large number of items, as well as with the European Economic Community through the Lomé agreement. As already mentioned, items excluded from the CBI and CARIBCAN were the result of business and political interests in both the US and Canada. The issue is not only one of obtaining access for the excluded items of CBI and CARIBCAN. If CARICOM countries were to offer reciprocal trade to the US, as suggested in the EAI, similar concessions would have to be extended to Canada also, since CARIBCAN commits Commonwealth Caribbean countries to extend to Canada any benefit extended to another developed country.[14] A similar clause also binds Caribbean countries under the Lomé Convention to offer to developed European countries any benefits offered other developed countries, such as the US and Canada.[15]

A further complication that CARICOM countries face is the extension of free access by the US to other Latin American countries not currently CBI beneficiaries. Such an extension, even if reciprocal, would reduce the level of preferences under the CBI.[16] CARICOM countries are not in a strong bargaining position because, unlike the Lomé Convention which is a negotiated agreement between beneficiary states and the European Economic Community, both the CBI and CARIBCAN are grants

---

[14] See Anthony Gonzales, "CARICOM Trade Agreements with the USA, Canada and the EEC: Issues of Compatibility and Trade Benefits in the Light of the Proposed EAI," Feb 2, 1991.

[15] Ibid.

[16] See CARICOM Document p.9, conversation with Mr. Isaacs of CARICOM and argument by Jeffrey Schott.

from the US and Canadian governments respectively, and as such may be withdrawn at any time.[17]

In addition to the above, there is no consensus in the region favouring two-way free trade. The larger CARICOM states appear more receptive to the idea, more particularly on a sector-by-sector basis.[18] While the sector-by-sector approach is favoured by some, it is acknowledged that this may be too drawn-out a process and might result in some of the same exclusions being made as are currently in place under the CBI. Jose Orive, Chairman of the CBI Embassy Group in Washington, insists that CBI countries are ready to move in the direction of free trade, even if it means lowering trade barriers in their own countries. However, at least one well-placed Washington Administration official believes that opening Caribbean economies would only benefit Caribbean countries marginally and that in the long run only Washington would benefit from a reciprocal regime.[19]

The smaller countries or less-developed members of the regional grouping are the most sceptical about the benefits of two-way trade with the US. "The United States needs nothing that we have to sell," said one St. Lucian agro-industrial entrepreneur. "They can produce just

---

[17] Ibid.

[18] This was revealed during my discussions with individuals, particularly in Jamaica and Trinidad and Tobago.

[19] See conversation with Ann Hughes of the US Commerce Dept in Editorial Research Report, Dec 8, 1989 pp. 682-692.

about everything we have to offer and much more cheaply."[20] Similar views were expressed by another industry executive in St. Lucia. The Pyramid Garments spokesperson pointed out that opening up the markets in these small countries in order to sell garments was highly risky. "The garment industry is highly mobile. They move from one island to another. Their major consideration is cheap labour and our people are no longer willing to do slave labour"[21].

Women's groups and non-government organizations (NGOs) in the region point to the Maquiladoras in Mexico and Free Trade Zones in the region as examples of free trade in action. The Maquiladoras are the approximately 2,000 plants along the US-Mexico border, the majority of which are US-owned. They employ 465,000 Mexican workers to assemble electronic, automotive and textile products for export to the US.[22] That model, they argue, is exploitive of women in particular and provides little long-term benefit to the countries within which those enclave economies operate.[23] Indeed, it is well-documented that the majority of low-paying jobs in the foreign-owned factories operating in Mexico are held by young, often unmarried women who work in lax environmental and often sub-

[20] Conversation with Mrs. Bonnie Zephrin of Viking Industries, Castries, St. Lucia, April 3, 1991.

[21] Conversation on April 3, 1991.

[22] See Time, June 3, 1991 p.53.

[23] Conversation with Mrs. Peggy Antrobus, Director of Women and Development Unit (WAND), University of the West Indies, Cavehill, Barbados, March 13, 1991.

standard social conditions. "The maquiladora program is a case study of the kinds of environmental catastrophes that can happen where trade and investment rule," says Stewart Hudson of the National Wildlife Federation.[24]

Representative John J. LaFalce, Democrat of New York, says that the rationale for Item 807 (the section of the US Tariff Code that permits Maquiladoras) is the survival of US industry. LaFalce holds that, in the face of today's intense international competition, many American firms can no longer compete with companies that use low-wage labour, unless they move their own labour-intensive operations to Mexico. According to LaFalce, "the choice is between assembling American-made parts in Mexico, thereby retaining some American jobs, or moving the entire manufacturing process further away".[25] In their effort to alleviate the debt crisis and attract more foreign investment, many countries in the region bend over backwards to make local conditions attractive to investors by not enforcing environmental or labour laws. These governments justify their position on the basis of the jobs that are provided. On the other hand, opponents argue that the minimal benefits of these measures will not contribute to long-term sustainable development.

The same sort of situation could be expected to develop in the Caribbean with the implementation of the EAI. Peggy Antrobus, Director of the Women and Development Unit (WAND) of the University of the West Indies in Barbados, says:

---

[24] See Time, June 3, 1991 p. 56.

[25] See Editorial Research Reports, Dec 8, 1989, p. 691.

> The assumptions of the dominant view (a view that is shared by Washington and most Caribbean governments today, but not by the Non-Government Organizations (NGOs) and WAND associated groups), is that you can exploit female services. Free Trade zones (FTZs) do this... When you promote FTZs you have no control over factors of labour. In the Caribbean there is a high import of products and we have little or no control. The only local content is labour and you have to push that as low as possible. If those factories were staffed by men the unions would never accept this.[26]

Antrobus says that FTZs have contributed to the restructuring of the labour force. The change that is occurring is from a high percentage of skilled female labourers to unskilled female labour. The result is that the level of wages throughout the whole society suffers, which also affects men. Antrobus adds that "If the reality is that you have to squeeze your labour force in order to benefit under the EAI then it is not worth it." In addition, Antrobus explains that in the Caribbean more and more people are losing jobs in the formal or manufacturing sector to the informal or unregulated sector. Increasing unemployment, she argues, leads to a lack of stability, which in turn leads to lack of investment.

Environmental factors also need to be considered. Critics like Antrobus hold that the lack of environmental laws will contribute to pollution and erode already poor health standards in most CARICOM countries.[27] The Free Trade model, according to the Non-Government Organizations (NGOs), only provides short-term measures which are likely to evolve into long-term problems. It provides "quick fixes for politicians who want to get

---

[26] Discussion held on March 13, 1991, Barbados.

[27] Antrobus, 1991.

reelected but the long-term effect of increased industrialization without adequate environmental protection could be negative."[28] Without careful planning, tourism, in which many of the countries share a comparative advantage, could be adversely affected. Unplanned development in that sector is already creating health and environmental problems for certain countries. Garbage and sewage disposal are two of the biggest problems confronting that industry.

Can local industries survive reciprocal free trade? Richard Taurel, a Barbadian manufacturer of plastic bottles, said that certain essential industries in the region needed to be given protection. Others, according to Taurel, need time to learn to compete within the region first before having to confront the extra-regional competition.[29] Mr. Taurel's view is shared by many individuals in the smaller islands, many of whom pointed to the lack of free trade within the Caribbean itself, a problem which needs to be rectified as a first step before wider free trade can be considered.

The problem of regional free trade is recognized. The Common External Tariff (CET), one of several initiatives designed to achieve regional free trade, is anticipated to be implemented by member countries during 1991 along with a set of Revised Rules of Origin. These measures are expected to provide protection for fledgling industries by providing a common tariff for extraregional trade, while lowering tariffs within the region itself. This protection, they argue, is necessary in order to build up the

[28] Ibid.

[29] Conversation with Mr. R. Taurel, Barbados, March, 1991.

strength of industries and to increase regional competitiveness before having to compete internationally.[30] The CET was given the approval of CARICOM Heads of Government some years ago but to date has only been implemented by some CARICOM countries, although all were expected to follow in 1991.

However, some people believe that the CET has little chance of success. Scepticism is based on the view that the policy has been implemented too late. Furthermore, the very notion of a protected area is in conflict with the concept of free trade, proposed in the EAI.[31] So while CARICOM countries are not collectively in favour of reciprocal trade, they are also doubtful that the measures which have been adopted to strengthen their economies will have more than a fighting chance of success.

The second component of the EAI, investment, has several implications. The EAI calls for the creation of a new investment sector loan program in the inter-American Development Bank (IDB) for nations that "take significant steps to remove impediments to international investment," and envisions that the program would likely work in conjunction with World Bank lending programmes.[32] Many CARICOM countries fear that this new role assigned to the IDB would have the effect of undermining the role of

---

[30] Conversation with Mr. Hayden Blades of CARICOM, Guyana, March, 1991.

[31] Discussions with Yesu Persad, Director of Demerara Distillers, Guyana, March, 1991 and Ian McDonald of the West Indian Commission, Guyana, March 1991.

[32] See EAI Statement, June 27, 1990.

the Caribbean Development Bank (CDB), to which all CARICOM countries have membership.

Analysis of the EAI requires some understanding of the role which the IDB is expected to play in the initiative. The IDB is the largest regional development bank. There are some 44 member countries, including 25 Latin American and Caribbean countries. However, not all CARICOM countries are members. The US is the Bank's largest shareholder.

A study undertaken in 1980 on the operations of the IDB pointed to the unique role of the US in that institution.[33] Because the US is the largest shareholder, it has the deciding vote. Thus, lending institutions such as the IDB are made to comply with US international monetary, fiscal and foreign policy. In addition, the structure and operations of the IDB is similar to that of other institutions such as the World Bank and the IMF.

The IDB has been assigned a key role in three of the EAI's components. Its resources are to be used to support commercial bank debt reduction. In addition, the Bank's tradition of supporting integration efforts in Latin America are to be expanded to support measures to increase trade. The Bank is also going to work with the Commission for Latin America and the Caribbean (CEPAL) to support efforts for training and

[33] See Sovani, Mahboob Ali, The Role of Regional Development Banks in the Integrative Process of Developing Countries - Case Study of the Inter-American Development Bank, 1980, p.75.

to assist regional governments which are "engaging in export expansion and trade negotiations."[34]

The Bank will also be involved in improving the business and investment climate in the region, and a policy framework is being developed to deal with investment and sector loans. Loans will likely be tied to the removal of impediments to business and investment. Obstacles which are likely to be identified, according to Dr. Hayes, the Bank's external relations advisor, are problems in domestic banking, tax structures, legal and regulatory requirements and commercial practices. The components of the policy framework are expected to be discussed with both the private and public sector.

Since its establishment in the 1960s, the Bank has lent close to $41 billion dollars to Latin American and Caribbean members and represented a corresponding $122 billion worth of investments. Between 1990 and 1993, the Bank proposes to lend roughly $22.5 billion, which will make it the largest source of new investment capital for countries in the region. Funds for the region are expected to be divided up as follows: sixty-five percent for the seven largest economies and 35 percent for the smaller and less-developed countries.[35] The latter represents a small increase from the previous replenishments. According to Dr. Hayes, twenty-five percent of the lending programme is earmarked for "fast disbursing sector loans which will be developed in tandem with the World Bank."

[34] Hayes, 1990:6.

[35] Ibid.

The IDB is expected to administer a proposed grant fund of $1.5 billion which would support private enterprise. There is a growing fear that the anticipated contribution of 1.5 billion dollars over five years to be funded jointly by the US, Japan and EEC will not be reached because of increasing demands by other regions, such as the Middle East for aid following the Iraq war, and the growing needs of Eastern Europe. There are reports that the Japanese are unhappy at the prospect of providing funding that will essentially be used to subsidize private enterprise.[36]

Furthermore, CARICOM countries have good reason to believe that the demand for funds will not be evenly met. At a recent meeting of the IDB in Japan, Mr. P. J. Patterson, Deputy Prime Minister of Jamaica, speaking on behalf of the CARICOM members of the Bank, Jamaica, Barbados, the Bahamas, Guyana, and Trinidad and Tobago, criticised the IDB for "failing to meet its commitments to smaller and poorer countries in the region." According to Mr. Patterson, "only 26 percent of the Bank's loans went to these smaller countries. A far cry from its target of 35 percent." Furthermore, according to the Jamaican Minister, "the bank's pledge to direct 50 percent of such loans to low-income groups was not met, amounting to only 41 percent which was below the 1989 level of 49 percent."[37] Thus, while the debt component of the EAI is of interest to certain countries, it is, like the trade component, regarded as having a

[36] This report was circulated during the IDB meeting in Japan in 1991, information based on discussion held at Mona, Jamaica, April 17, 1991.

[37] Kal Wagenheim, Caribbean Update, Vol 7, No 4, (New Jersey: May 1991), p.1.

limited impact on CARICOM countries. The EAI has proposed to handle concessional and commercial debt to the US separately.[38] The US recognition of the debt problem as a serious one for the Caribbean, particularly in the case of Jamaica and Guyana is viewed positively by the region. They are, however, somewhat wary of the proposal to reduce Latin American and Caribbean official debt by tying debt relief to "countries that adopt strong economic and investment reform programmes with the support of international institutions."[39] While the US administration has acknowledged that a certain degree of flexibility must be permitted individual countries in order to avoid "serious adverse impacts on the poor and on the environment as a result of World Bank and IMF structural adjustment programs,"[40] nevertheless, the basic criteria which Latin American or Caribbean countries must meet in order to qualify for debt reduction benefits is essentially the structural adjustment model.

The term 'structural adjustment' refers to the package of IMF stabilization policies for short-run balance of payments adjustment, as well as a commitment to diversifying exports. The term has also been described as "austerity plus export diversification."[41] These policies have been recommended to Caribbean states since 1974, by a number of international

---

[38] CARICOM document p.9.

[39] Ibid.

[40] See Enterprise for the Americas Initiative Act of 1990, Oct. 22, 1990, 101st Congress 2nd Session House of Reps. Report 101-917, p.2.

[41] Carmen Diana Deere et al., In the Shadow of the Sun, (Boulder, Colorado: Westview Press, 1990), pp.18 and 44.

organizations such as the International Monetary Fund (IMF). However, these policies are widely considered to have caused deterioration in conditions rather than the sustained growth they were designed to encourage.[42]

Mike McCormack of the Council of Churches and Human Rights Association of Guyana points out that the essential dilemma for industrial countries is that their bilateral and multilateral programmes conflict.[43] For instance, Canada's bilateral programme in Guyana considers social issues but the multilateral programmes adopt structural adjustment. According to McCormack there is a fundamental contradiction because the multilateral programme is designed to cut back on public spending, remove subsidies and the like, while bilateral programmes support very opposite initiatives. McCormack points to a new bilateral Canadian initiative in Guyana called the 'Futures programme,' which aids rural groups to become more self-sufficient in agriculture. It is designed to soften the impact of the structural adjustment programme which the Guyanese government has adopted, with the encouragement and full support of Canada. McCormack argues that structural adjustment has negative impacts on the people who are least qualified to undergo the adjustments, that is, the very poor.

---

[42] The Spectrum "Structural Adjustment Has not Helped" Vol. 6 No. 5, (Ottawa: May l5, l989), p.3.

[43] Conversation with McCormack on March 27, Georgetown, Guyana, 1991.

In any case, until the fundamental problem of a corrupt and inefficient political system is addressed, the programmes will not have the desired effect.[44] Programmes like Futures may have a chance of success if control is exercised by NGOs and not by the government. In other words, according to McCormack, all such programmes would be more successful if they had long-term rather than short-term goals.

But structural adjustment cannot be blamed for everything. For instance, although Delisle Worrell, a Director of the Central Bank of Barbados, attributes some blame to the structural adjustment problem which he says has had negative social effects in places like Guyana, he argues that it is simplistic to put all the blame on such programmes: "That strand of criticism doesn't take account of the lack of human and financial resources needed to keep countries like Guyana afloat. Even when you do get sufficient finance, there is not the human resources."[45] Worrell says that even the most hard-pressed governments have tried to cut education and health last of all. He holds that the regional ideology is against cutting those types of services. However, according to Worrell, it would be better to make rational cuts in order to maintain certain services at a healthy level, rather than keep underfunded facilities in operation.

While external circumstances contributed to the regional economic crisis, domestic economies have to share some of the blame.

---

[44] Ibid.

[45] Discussion with Delisle Worrell of the Central Bank of Barbados (CBB) on April 8th, 1991, Barbados. The views of Delisle Worrell are his personal views and should not be attributed to the Central Bank of Barbados. Discussion on April 8, Barbados, 1991.

Worrell attributes the weak economies on poor conditions in the seventies and eighties, however, "we would not have done so badly if we had managed resources more prudently. In effect our economies are open and there is a reluctance to accept the interactions between ourselves and North America."[46]

Still, the effects of structural adjustment programmes have been severe in many places. For instance, Caribbean states paid 160 million dollars more as debt payments to the IMF in 1986 than they received in loans. Similarly, the region paid out 92.6 million US dollars more in interest on loans than it received in grants and loans from all sources.[47] A Conference of Non-Government Organizations meeting in St. George's, Grenada in April 1989, organized by the Caribbean People's Development Agency (CARIPEDA), concluded that "whilst governments tout figures of increased growth, the condition of Caribbean people has worsened."[48] These policies are considered to have served to increase the gap between the rich and poor.

This same group concluded by expressing its concern about "increased domination and control of the planning process in the region by foreign experts."[49] Indeed, Caribbean countries may have to accept certain conditions which touch on domestic policies and strike at their

---

[46] Ibid.

[47] Ibid.

[48] Ibid.

[49] Ibid.

sovereignty as part of a *quid pro quo* for getting to the free trade table, much as Canada and Mexico have had to do. Canada made important changes to its energy policy prior to free trade negotiations, while Mexico has undertaken a bold series of reforms designed to liberalise its economy prior to free trade negotiations with the US. In fact, the EAI provides for priority to be given to countries which undertake "important policy reforms." Other support is intended for agriculture and infrastructure related projects.

The IDB would also impose structural adjustment lending. Indeed, some regional analysts believe its terms would be as severe as that of the IMF and the World Bank, with an added requirement that would have to do with private investment.[50] Professor Kari Levitt, an international economist and Caribbean expert, who has written on the effect of structural adjustment in the Caribbean, says: "The IDB will impose very specific conditions having to do with the sale of government assets, such as the Jamaica National Bank, all government holdings and a whole list of other government assets." Furthermore, she argues that "the loan forgiveness is not operational, unless these conditions are met. A large proportion of IDB funds will be made available for countries which are 'on board.' In contrast, Canada wrote off the debt of the Caribbean."[51] So, while the debt component of the EAI is of interest to certain countries, it is unlikely to benefit the majority of CARICOM countries.

[50] Discussion with Prof. Kari Levitt, Caribbean Analyst and resident tutor at the Consortium School of Graduate Studies, U.W.I. Mona, Jamaica, April, 17, 1991.

[51] Ibid.

Some people believe that the EAI promotes a US agenda. Peggy Antrobus holds that the EAI is really about a dominant ideological model. Antrobus says that, like IMF policies, the EAI is designed to restructure the economies of the region in a new world order:

> The new world order spoken of by President Bush means that certain countries will have to be prepared to sink...The only way in which one can understand this is to understand the US need to expand its power. They are all saying to the Caribbean that the only way to expand is to buy into free trade... the EAI is not intended to benefit the Caribbean or Latin America. It will benefit US industry and multinational companies (MNCs).

However, Antrobus acknowledges that her view is considered the alternative, rather than the dominant, perspective in the region.

According to Worrell, too much attention is being placed on the new Bush Initiative: "A lot of the efforts we are employing towards the EAI are somewhat misplaced. We should be concentrating on improving existing agreements but the US pushed the EAI to a great deal...that is why everyone is preoccupied with it." Worrell adds:

> I see the EAI as operating at different levels of interest and can be implemented through other mechanisms requiring changes in tariffs. This is going to be an untidy process and will take some time. The only country likely to benefit from the EAI, within CARICOM, is Jamaica, which will get some debt relief. The US will probably insist that the others pay their debts.

> By the time they get to Brazil and Argentina, there will probably not be much left for others.[52]

Neither the trade nor the investment components of the EAI are new. The trade and investment components are similar to previous plans. CBI I and II offered one-way free trade in several sectors but ended up excluding items such as the garment industry and sugar that were of real interest to CARICOM countries. At a time when Caribbean economies face the greatest uncertainty, the EAI is proposing that they consider opening up their fragile markets to reciprocal trade. By extending CBI privileges to EAI beneficiaries, large Latin American countries like Brazil will benefit at the expense of the smaller Caribbean markets. With no guarantee that the promised investments funds will be committed, the EAI is seen by some regional politicians as suffering from the same omission as its predecessor, the CBI. Its so-called investment sector is practically non-existent.

The only new aspects of the EAI are its debt reduction plan and the notion of tying a portion of its relief to an environment fund. But, as was earlier noted, only a few Caribbean countries have the type and level of debt so as to benefit from the EAI provisions. Moreover, the conditions that are likely to be applied to debt relief have the potential of infringing on the right of member countries to pursue national objectives. Some regional analysts believe that the conditions proposed under the EAI are likely to undermine the democratic process. Agreements which commit governments to cut social and other essential services, while assisting the

[52] Worrell, April 8, Barbados, 1991.

private sector, amounts to tying the hands of politicians and preventing them from carrying out the programmes which they were elected to perform.[53] Although the EAI appears to fall short in fulfilling the needs of CARICOM countries, nevertheless, countries in the region feel obliged to give the Initiative serious consideration. "The EAI is central," says Mr. Ian MacDonald, a member of the West Indian Commission, because:

> The Caribbean is not of such strategic concern to the US today as a result of the lessening of East West tensions. The result is we will be forgotten. The Americans are more likely to put their energies into Mexico and some of the larger Latin American countries.[54]

According to MacDonald, there are important items for CARICOM countries to consider. The first is the need to get greater strength from deepening the regional approach, that is, among CARICOM countries. The second has to do with the need to widen the concept of Caribbean regionalization to include countries like the Dominican Republic, Haiti and even Cuba (if and when things change there). In other words, says MacDonald, "the Caribbean should begin to look at itself as a population of about 30 million people, instead of 5 million, by looking beyond the English speaking countries."[55]

---

[53] Conversation with Rosina Wiltshire-Brodber, Barbados: August, 1991.

[54] Conversation with Mr. Ian MacDonald, member of the West Indian Commission, Guyana: April, 1991.

[55] Ibid.

Not only will this increase the viability of the region, but this will also increase the region's voice internationally. Lester Bird, former Deputy Prime Minister of Antigua, adds that Prime Minister Brian Mulroney had advised the Caribbean Heads of Government at a meeting in Barbados in March 1990, to join the NAFTA or accept that the region would become additionally marginalised.[56] Bird adds that the Caribbean really has been left little choice. The overriding question to be explored in the next chapter is whether the region will face the challenge divided or united.

[56] Conversation with Lester Bird, Antigua, March, 1991.

Chapter 3

The Problems of Regional Integration: Why the Commonwealth Caribbean Faces Few Choices

Since the dissolution of the West Indian Federation in 1962, Caribbean countries have concentrated more heavily on economic than on political issues. But the looming NAFTA and its extension in the form of the EAI have once again brought the politics of the region into sharp focus. One analyst says that he believes the NAFTA and its extension in the form of the EAI has really caught regional politicians (figuratively speaking) "with their pants down." They were just beginning to assess the impact of the Canada/US free trade agreement (FTA), and now they have to face the added challenge of Mexico and perhaps other more-developed Latin American countries. In analyzing the strengths and weaknesses of the EAI, it is important to assess the political position of the Commonwealth Caribbean. There is a general assessment by regional analysts that the countries are vulnerable to the changing international economic order, not only because they remain economically weak but because they are so politically divided.

The case for regional integration in the Caribbean is hardly new; however, it is gaining new converts in light of the challenges facing the area. It has been suggested that the Caribbean had three options to pursue: independence; regional integration; or satellite status (Cuba/USSR relations).[1] However, Cuba's uncertain future due to changes in world economic relations and the realignment of political forces indicates that the third option is fading fast. Indeed, the future of the first option is just as doubtful. Some two decades after independence most Caribbean countries, including the more developed, have been unable to achieve any significant degree of economic self-determination. [2] Thus, the region appears to have been left with only one viable option.

One argument made by those favouring regional integration is that the Caribbean will need, at the very least, highly skilled negotiators in talks with the United States (US). At best, a united position on issues that are important to the region is generally considered to be a goal worth pursuing. It is also well known that for logistic reasons the US would prefer to deal with groups of countries rather than single ones (the only exceptions to this appear to be Canada, Mexico and some believe possibly Chile).

In this chapter we will look at the political obstacles to regional integration in the Commonwealth Caribbean. It is posited here that integration is not just a function of regional economic considerations, but that it depends on political initiatives and the active participation of the people of the region for it to work. Integration is a process which consists

---

[1] Jennifer Hosten-Craig, "CARIBCAN: An Analysis and Alternative Solutions," Ottawa: (1989), unpublished paper for Carleton Univ.

[2] First Progress Report of the West Indian Commission, Barbados: 1991, introduction.

of a growing social, cultural, economic and political interaction among peoples, the object of which is to enhance sovereignty and cultural identity.[3] The first part of the paper will consider the theoretical justification for 'unity.' The reasons for the failure of the West Indies federation will then be reviewed in order to make the point that many of those reasons were political. The third section will briefly explore some of the problems facing the region today and attempt to demonstrate why regional integration is the only way to face the challenges of a new international economic order. In conclusion, I hope to demonstrate that political considerations are certainly as important as economic ones in forging greater regional unity and a regional identity.

The justification for integration is based on two principal considerations. The first of these is 'power' and the second is the need for a 'West Indian identity.'[4] William Demas, the noted Caribbean economist and integrationist, has pointed to the importance of the phenomenon of 'power' in international relations. As he explains, power is not a commodity but rather a dynamic set of relationships; Relationships of super-ordination and subordination, of dominance and dependence, dominate relations between many industrialized countries and less-developed countries.

Because of the predominance of power relationships, what really counts is not formal sovereignty but 'effective' sovereignty. According to Demas, effective sovereignty would increase the power of

---

[3] Girvan, 1990: 4.

[4] See William Demas, "Development, Identity and Unity in the Caribbean" in West Indian Nationhood and Caribbean Integration, ed. David I. Mitchell (CCC Publishing House, Barbados: 1974) p.7.

countries like those of the Caribbean giving them greater strength to pursue national objectives.[5] Thus, small fragmented Commonwealth Caribbean countries should seek to increase their 'effective' sovereignty. This is particularly true of the small Eastern Caribbean countries. One effort towards this end would be to pool the region's bargaining power by surrendering a part of its formal sovereignty. This would serve to increase the effective sovereignty of the collective bargaining unit. By integrating in some form, small countries can act as a large country with an enhanced ability to influence. The pooling of power can be effectively implemented in a number of bargaining situations as well as within international organizations. For instance, one of the reasons for the formation of the European Community was to improve its bargaining position vis-à-vis the US.[6]

This pooling of power has been one of the most significant arguments in favour of regional integration. It was also the rationale which drew Caribbean states together to form the Caribbean Free Trade Agreement (CARIFTA) in 1968, the precursor to the Caribbean Community (CARICOM), to successfully negotiate the Lomé agreements with the European Economic Commission. The Lomé Convention currently governs

---

[5] Ibid. p.7.

[6] Yarbrough and Yarbrough, <u>The World Economy: Trade and Finance</u>, Chicago: The Dryden Press (1989), p.71.

economic co-operation between Europe and a number of African, Caribbean and Pacific (ACP) countries. It had its origin in France's desire to preserve its economic ties with its colonies during discussions leading to the formation of the European Economic Community. At the insistence of France, Part IV, Articles 131-136 was included in the Rome Treaty which was signed in 1958. This section committed the original six European members to associate a number of overseas countries and territories. The first, Lomé Convention, signed in Lomé (the capital of Togo) was the result of negotiations between European member countries and the ACP group.[7] It and subsequent agreements laid down the basis for co-operation between the European member countries and the ACP group of former colonies. While CARIFTA was thought useful in that it brought Caribbean countries together and thus strengthened the negotiating position of the region, it was later felt that a greater effort to co-ordinate the region's affairs was necessary. CARICOM replaced CARIFTA in 1973 with the signing of the Treaty of Chaguaramas. It is intended to incrementally increase integrative measures over time. The current level of economic stability currently achieved by most of the CARICOM Less-Developed States (LDCs) has been attributed to a number of coordinated policies. The regional sub-grouping, known as the Organization of Eastern Caribbean States (OECS), has embarked on a number of common policies, including a common currency and diplomatic representation, and such measures as bulk buying,

[7] See Ramesh Ramsaran, The Commonwealth Caribbean in the World Economy, London: Macmillan Caribbean (1989), pp.133-134.

in order to minimize costs and maximize benefits. In addition, they are currently considering the feasibility of political union.

The power consideration is but one dimension of the challenge posed by the EAI and changing international economic order. The other concerns the question of a West Indian identity. While the EAI recognizes that the English-speaking Caribbean countries are within America's sphere of influence as well as that of the countries of Latin America, it challenges them to not only increase their bargaining power but prevent the erosion of their West Indian identity. Professor Norman Girvan, another regional expert, says that the bargaining challenge posed by the EAI is beyond the capacity of the CARICOM group and requires a wider regional grouping.[8] It has become more difficult to focus attention on the English-speaking countries since the Caribbean region was redefined by US officials as the Caribbean basin, which includes the island countries as well as all those Central American countries whose shores are washed by the Caribbean sea.[9] Thus, it can be anticipated that any effort to formally enlarge the CARICOM grouping by including non-English-speaking states such as the Dominican Republic will tend to further dilute the already fragile alliance of English-speaking countries. More importantly, it poses a substantive challenge to the shared historical and cultural heritage derived

---

[8] See Introduction in Integration and Participatory Development A Selection of Papers from the Second Conference of Caribbean Economists, ed. Judith Wedderburn, Bridgetown, Barbados, May 1990, p.4.

[9] See the CBI legislation.

from colonialism, which gave birth to the present concept of a West Indian identity.

The fragmented and individualistic nature of English-speaking Caribbean countries makes them particularly vulnerable to the loss of their West Indian identity. William Demas makes the distinction between personal and national or regional identity. For our purpose only group identity, as in national or regional identity, is considered relevant. Group identity is important because it generates self-confidence and self-worth. These are important components of development, particularly on the part of underdeveloped former colonial states.[10] Clive Thomas and other Dependency theorists have explained how psychological, cultural and intellectual dependence can impact negatively on development in regions like the Caribbean and Latin America.[11]

West Indians do share an identity. Although they share certain values with their neighbours in North and South America, they have, at the same time, most in common with each other. They share a history, music and language, as well as generally similar ethnic heritage, values and societal norms. However, the types of identity which developmental specialists consider essential are those that seek to develop indigenous institutions, or those that are locally molded, even if externally influenced, as well as having their own values, standards and societal norms. There are other ingredients of a cultural identity but it is sufficient for the purposes

[10] See Demas, 1974: pp 3-7.

[11] See Clive Y. Thomas, "From Colony to State Capitalism: Alternative Paths of Development in the Caribbean." Transition 5 (1982): 1-20.

of this paper to identify 'identity' as an important component of development. Furthermore, it is recognized that this is an area in which there is much room for improvement on the part of Commonwealth Caribbean countries.

CARICOM countries will need to work twice as hard to protect their regional identity under a free-trade regime. It is generally recognized that identity results from successfully solving one's own problems by one's own methods[12]. This is less likely to be the case under a free-trade regime, as described under the EAI. The freeing of trade and the conditions of debt relief and investment, as earlier described, all imply much less internal control than was previously the case.

Furthermore, the chances of preserving a West Indian identity is less likely while Caribbean people remain divided and fragmented. Indeed, one of the arguments made by Canada in favour of trilateral negotiations with the US and Mexico is that a three-way deal will preclude the possibility of a situation in which the US has the upperhand and overall advantage in those negotiations. Had trilateral negotiations not been agreed to, the US would have been the only country with free access to both the Canadian and Mexican economies, a situation which would have enhanced the investment climate in the US at the expense of Canada and increased the US bargaining position. It is noteworthy that Canadian cultural protection remains one of the only issues that the Canadian government has been adamant in excluding from the North American Free Trade Agreement (NAFTA) bargaining table. Not only is Canadian culture

[12] Demas, 1974: 4.

threatened by the increased influence of its giant neighbour to the south, but it is also politically recognized that certain institutions and businesses, such as the Canadian Broadcasting Corporation and publishing companies, are the glue for keeping as diverse a country as Canada together. If not excluded from the bargaining table, these industries would be forced to compete with their American counterparts on purely 'bottom line' considerations, which could, over time, undermine Canadian unity and identity.

But do Caribbean countries recognize the importance of 'unity' as a crucial variable in increasing their bargaining power, and of curtailing the potential erosion of a Caribbean or West Indian identity, as we now know it? Studies have been undertaken to discern the cause of the dissolution of the West Indian federation in 1962.[13] Just recently, however, a study was commissioned by Caribbean Heads of Government and CARICOM that will have a much wider mandate than previous studies. The West Indian Commission will explore public opinion in the region on ways to foster greater integration in the face of formidable challenges confronting the region in the 1990s. It is headed by well-known West Indian statesman, Sir Shidrath (Sonny) Ramphal, former Secretary General of the Commonwealth. The work of the Commission is assisted by a number of well-known Caribbean academics and personalities. The work of the Commission is being regarded with healthy scepticism on the part of some regional observers as just another in a series of endless studies which are never acted upon. Others see the Commission as an appropriate body

[13] See Etzioni, 1965.

whose time has come. The Commission, in recognition of the possible political ramifications of its conclusions, has chosen to seek its funding from outside of the region in order to preserve its independence. Any suggestions regarding the process of integration are likely to be highly political.

The problems facing the Caribbean today are many and stand in the way of integration. They include lack of capital, growing unemployment, low technological levels, inadequately developed infrastructure, lack of management skills, low resource bases, with the exception of the more developed countries of Trinidad, Guyana and Jamaica, and transportation. These problems have taken on greater importance, not only because of the general uncertainty and pessimism surrounding the performance of the world economy, but also because of the anticipated long-term technological and demographic changes which are likely to affect "the actual and potential demand for Caribbean exports, as well as...the growing multipolarity in international economic relationships." According to Alister McIntyre, a leading Caribbean economist, these trends indicate the need for different strategies than those so far pursued by the region; countries will "have to transform their patterns of development from one centred around the utilization of natural resources, to one relying on the utilization and upgrading of human resources."[14] Many people believe that it would be easier to develop a strategy for maximizing the region's resources if the countries were more united.

---

[14] See Development in Suspense: Selected Papers and Proceedings of the First Conference of Caribbean Economists eds. George Beckford and Norman Girvan pub. Friedrich Ebert Stiftung, Jamaica, 1989, p. 1X.

Others point to the disadvantages for developing countries of political unification. For instance, the question of distribution of industries across member countries has been a problem, especially among groups of developing countries which are anxious to industrialize. This issue was a major factor in the failure of the Central American Common Market established in the 1960s.[15] Indeed, the history of integration among developing countries shows that most have failed within ten years of their establishment. The relative longevity of CARICOM, therefore, provides some room for optimism.

A recent analysis of the integration effort in the Commonwealth Caribbean countries concludes that the experience has been positive. According to Vincent McDonald, a professor of Economics at Howard University, the Commonwealth Caribbean has been the recipient of net benefits from integration efforts. McDonald points to the formation of the Organization of Eastern Caribbean States under the aegis of CARICOM. In addition, over time a number of regional institutions have been put in place, and while there is room for improvement, inter-regional trade has increased. McDonald believes that there is an urgent need, in light of the new groupings which are taking place between developed countries, for politicians in the region to move to harmonize regional policy.[16]

---

[15] See Yarbrough and Yarbrough, The World Economy: Trade and Finance. Chicago: The Dryden Press, (1989), p. 71.

[16] Vincent R. McDonald, "Regional Cooperation: Panacea for Self-Sustaining Growth," Paper prepared for presentation at XV Annual CSA Conference, Trinidad and Tobago, May 22-24,(1990), p.16.

While greater integration is unlikely to solve all of the problems, many believe that it could go a long way towards alleviating the region's problems. One regional journalist says that "the problem of the Caribbean is that they cannot see that their future lies in political unification."[17] The greatest degree of unity has been achieved by the LDCs (St. Vincent and the Grenadines, St. Lucia, Grenada, Dominica, Antigua and Barbuda, Montserrat, St. Kitts and Nevis). In the past few years the strength of LDC economies has caused regional observers to reconsider the assignment of certain countries to the categories of "less developed" and "more developed."

The question of integration in the wider CARICOM sense, however, remains as fraught with problems as in the past. The short-lived West Indian Federation (1958-1962) failed for a number of reasons. Although economic reasons were an important aspect, factors such as the "meagre" administrative structure and the paucity of its finances, were significant reasons.[18] There were also important political reasons for the federation's failure. Among the most important reasons was the elite driven politics of the leadership and their lack of political will. This was evident in the actions of two of Jamaica's leading federal politicians, Norman Manley and Alexander Bustamante, both of whom "were primarily oriented to island politics, as is evident in their unwillingness to resign their island offices in

[17] Conversation with Mr. Leslie Pierre, editor of The Grenadian Voice, St. George's, Grenada, August 2nd, 1991.

[18] See Amitai Etzioni, Political Unification; A Comparative Study of Leaders and Forces, pub. Holt, Rinehart and Winston, Inc., New York, 1965, p. 154.

order to seek federal office."[19] Notable exceptions were Sir Grantley Adams of Barbados and T. Albert Marryshow of Grenada, both of whom saw the virtues of federation and were prepared to move out from their own island influence and inspire others with their vision of the region.

Other political reasons for the failure of the West Indies Federation included the regional balance of power and the problems of freedom of movement, transportation, and low and declining identification with the region. Briefly, the problem of the balance of power was manifested at two levels. In the first level, the main difficulty was the disparity between the more-developed countries and the smaller LDCs. The political structure that was designed for the West Indies federation by the British government took into account the weakness of the LDCs (these countries are not only smaller but lack mineral resources). Accordingly, the British government assigned a higher level of representation from the LDCs in the federal structure of the federation. The rationale for these 'corrective mechanisms' was the need to provide "a basis for a more stable integrative arrangement in that they represent an attempt to create conditions of industrialization and development at the poles of stagnation in the region."[20] However, these arrangements were unacceptable to the larger more developed countries (MDCs), in particular, Jamaica, which had the largest population and which believed it would lose politically as well as economically.

---

[19] Etzioni, 1965: 156.

[20] Andrew Axline, Caribbean Integration: The Politics of Regionalism, pub. Frances Pinter Ltd., London: pub. Frances Pinter Lte. (1979), p.69.

A further problem arose from the geopolitics of the region. The site chosen to be the capital city was Port-of-Spain, Trinidad. This choice was largely based on Trinidad's closer proximity to the other countries in the union. Jamaica, in contrast, is located much further away. Thus, Jamaica felt challenged, first by what it felt was unfair representation by the LDCs and, secondly, by the additional advantage given to Trinidad, which it tended to view as a competitor. When these political factors were added to the domestic political scene, the result was a simmering brew resulting in the union's eventual dissolution.

Both Jamaicans and Trinidadians also feared competition from lower-paid labour from the small islands.[21] It was thought in some circles that loosening immigration restrictions between the islands would result in the arrival of hoards of immigrant workers from the LDCs to work in the more-developed islands. Needless to say, local opposition parties seized this opportunity to garner support for their own political ends and in the process undermined the spirit and goals of the federation.

Transportation problems have always plagued the region. During federation the Canadian government, in recognition of this fact, gave a gift of two ships to the union. The' Federal Palm' and the 'Federal Maple' are still fondly remembered by West Indians long after they have ceased to ply Caribbean waters. Transportation links by air and sea were greater between the islands and Britain and the US than between the member countries themselves during the federation. And it is still necessary for travellers from the islands to fly to Miami first in order to get to the Bahamas

[21] Etzioni: 167.

or Jamaica. This pattern of transportation is another example of how colonial dependence on a more developed country tends to persist after independence. However, this dependence has shifted from Great Britain to the Caribbean's closest neighbour, the US.

Indeed, it should be noted that the influence of the US on Caribbean countries had begun to grow in relation to that of Britain since before the collapse of the federation. In his analysis of why the federation failed, Amitai Etzioni points out that the larger islands of Jamaica and Trinidad were being drawn increasingly into the American economic orbit. In Jamaica the commercial mining of bauxite was given a boost from 1952 onwards. The development was the work of three foreign companies, two of which were American and one Canadian.[22] The result was a Jamaican economy which became heavily influenced by the bauxite industry and thus oriented towards North America, rather than towards Europe. Thus, although Jamaica was still dependent on British aid at the time of federation, it was less influenced by Britain than at previous periods in its history.

Similarly, Trinidad's economy, which is petroleum driven, nearly doubled between 1954 and 1960. Prior to that, Trinidad depended on Britain to purchase, at a high preferential rate, its sugar crop, which represented a high percentage of the island's export total. However, between 1954 and 1960 there was a sharp decline in agricultural exports with a corresponding rise in oil exports. Thus, in 1960 the Gross Domestic Product (GDP) of agricultural exports had declined to 13 percent, of which

---

[22] Elzioni: 162.

sugar accounted for only 8 percent, while petroleum products amounted to over 80 percent of the country's exports.[23] Significant financial assistance was made available to Trinidad, both through its petroleum industry, as well as through the US naval base at Chaguaramas, Trinidad. Consequently, like Jamaica, Trinidad was being more and more influenced by North America. What is even more significant, is that the influence that the US gained from its economic activity was subsequently exerted to influence political events and preserve American strategic interests in the Caribbean region. This was evident in the Grenada and Panama invasions, as well as in other US activities in Nicaragua and other parts of Central America. Other countries in the region have also been heavily influenced by American aid and tourism.[24]

Despite the above, which is not exclusive of other factors, some analysts have argued that a stronger sense of regional identification might have saved the West Indies Federation. According to David Lowenthal, who has written extensively about the region, West Indians generally have a narrow view of the region. "For West Indians...the island is in most contexts the most compelling area symbol. A man who says 'I am a Jamaican, or I am a Barbadian,' is very likely expressing the broadest allegiance he knows."[25] One of the only exceptions to this, according to

---

[23] The Trinidad Scene: A Prosperous Approach to Independence in Financial Times, June 29, 1962 in Etzioni, p. 164.

[24] Ibid.

[25] David Lowenthal, "The Social Background of West Indian Federation," in The West Indies Federation : Perspectives on a New Nation ed. David Lowenthal, 1961 Pub. The Columbia Univ. Press, New York, p.98.

Lowenthal, is when the combined West Indian cricket team plays against an outside team.[26] Over the years, this fact has not changed. More recently some of the OECS countries, having attained a slightly higher level of development, are showing signs of becoming smug and insular.[27] It has been noted that the greatest attachment to the concept of West Indian nationality is held by the educated middle class. Springer points out that many of the region's leaders, as well as teachers, intellectuals and technocrats, shared common experiences abroad in places like England, Canada and the US, to which they travelled to further their education.[28] Thus, an educated Jamaican often has more in common with an educated Grenadian than with an uneducated Jamaican.[29]

Although there is a certain degree of affinity among members of the working class in the region, this has been tempered by economic and political factors. As previously noted, some Jamaicans and Trinidadians feared competition from lower-paid 'small islanders.' This fear was exaggerated by opposition parties and organized labour, in order to protect narrow political and local interests.[30]

---

[26] Ibid.

[27] These opinions were recorded by the author during extensive interviews with a variety of people in the region.

[28] Springer, West Indies Emergent in Etzioni, p. 167.

[29] Ibid.

[30] See Etzioni: p. 167.

Some regional analysts believe that more could have been done by politicians to educate their populations about the advantages of labour mobility in the region. It is clear that the West Indian Federation lacked broad-based support. Most analysts note that public support could have been developed through regional political groupings which might have vigorously promoted the goals of a West Indian identity. Some of the same charges are made today and the Caribbean seems no better placed to deal with the political challenges to the region.

It is felt that the countries by and large are ill prepared for the challenge of free trade. Local attitudes are believed to be one of the biggest obstacles in the way of progress towards competitive and efficient economies. This stems from a neglect by politicians to speak honestly with their constituents. "They are reluctant to level with the people about the true economic state of the economies and they raise false hopes about their ability to solve the problems. As a result there are unrealistic expectations of governments."[31] This view accords with a recent economic assessment conducted by Anthony Boatswain of the region, in which he says: "There is definitely too much of a 'dependency syndrome'... dependence on Government for social amenities and job creation, dependence on private entrepreneurs for employment, dependence on external private investors to stimulate economic activities ...it is necessary to change this 'dependent' attitude and rely more on creative energies in forging an economic path to

[31] Conversation with Mrs. Joan Purcell, Minister of Tourism, Government of Grenada, Grenada, July 31, 1991.

higher levels of development and material welfare."[32] One top airline executive told me that the Caribbean may benefit in the long run, from the 'hard times' that many predict for the region. Hard times, according to this view, may help to change the laissez faire and careless attitude to education, training and service which tends to be predominant. The blame, he felt, belonged to politicians and the people collectively. A former politician stated that regional politicians are too preoccupied with being reelected to really get down to preparing their constituents to confront the developmental challenges they face through adequate education and training.[33]

With so much yet to put in place, the question of whether Caribbean countries are ready to accept two-way free trade with developed and developing neighbours in North and South America takes on added importance. To most observers, the Caribbean appears to have already accepted the EAI challenge. On July 22, 1991, in Washington, D.C. the Caribbean Community signed a CARICOM-United States Council Agreement on Trade and Investment with the government of the United States. The objectives of this multilateral framework agreement is contained in Article Two of the agreement:

> I) To monitor trade and investment relations, identify opportunities for

---

[32] See "An Economic Perspective: Attitude and Development by Anthony Boatswain in Business Eye, February/March, 1991 pub. Business Eye Int. Ltd, Grenada, p.15.

[33] Mr. Hugh Marshall, former Minister of Trade, government of Antigua, April, 1991.

expanding trade and investment and negotiate agreements where appropriate;

2) To hold consultations on specific trade and investment matters of interest to the Parties; and

3) To identify and work towards the removal of impediments to, and problems affecting, trade and investment flows.[34]

Articles three and four state the composition of the 'Council,' as well as meeting times. CARICOM is to be represented by the Chairperson of the Conference of Heads of government or an appropriate delegated official, and the US will be represented by the office of the US Trade Representatives. Meetings are to be held with the concurrence of both sides. Other articles of the agreement lay down other terms of reference, such as the scope of the Agreement and its accordance with other international obligations by both sides.[35]

The framework agreement calls for an "Immediate Action Agenda" which includes the discussion of Caribbean participation in the EAI. However, it is important to note that it does not commit CARICOM countries to accept a two-way free trade regime at this time. (This point was stressed by most officials with whom I spoke in the Caribbean). In

[34] See Agreement Between the Caribbean Community (CARICOM) and the Government of the United States of America concerning a CARICOM-US Council on Trade and Investment dated July 22nd, 1991, p.5.

[35] Ibid.

fact, article seven of the Agreement recognizes the presence of other regional and international arrangements (such as those between CARICOM countries and with the European Economic Commission (EEC)), as well as between the US and its other trading partners.

The fact that all CARICOM countries were signatories to the multilateral framework agreement does not mean that they commonly share an homogenous position on free trade or the other 'pillars' of the EAI. Rather, the limited agreement is dictated only by the recognized weakness of the region and the need of the countries to maintain good relations with the US. The region's weakness in dealing with its more-developed North American neighbours was reflected in this quotation by the President of the Caribbean Development Bank who said: "The EAI is like a ship setting sail. Although you don't know where it's going, you know that you have to get on. If you get on you can at least try to steer the ship but, if you don't, all you can do is stand on the shore and wave to those on board."[36]

This implied lack of control over one's destiny relates back to the two elements of power and identity with which I began the chapter. As earlier identified, the common element is the 'unity' component. Unity builds strength, particularly for small, economically vulnerable CARICOM economies. Jamaica, it seems, has finally recognized this fact, at least with respect to its bargaining position. This is evident in its decision to abandon negotiations with the US for a bilateral framework agreement in favour of a multilateral one which includes all members of the Caribbean Community.

[36] Conversation with Sir Neville Nichols, in Mexico, 1991 [36]1238

But to what extent will this fragile multilateral coalition hold in the long-term free-trade process envisioned between the region and North America? The coalition is described as 'fragile' because there appears to be more support for the free-trade component, by far the most important part of the EAI, by the CARICOM MDCs than by the LDCs. While most CARICOM officials believe that the multilateral framework agreement provides an opportunity for on-going discussion between CARICOM members and the US, there is less consensus regarding the actual benefits of the EAI.

The difference of opinion on the subject of the EAI exemplifies some of the attitudes earlier discussed. Elites in Jamaica, Guyana and Trinidad seemed generally resigned to the fact that the Caribbean market could only be protected for so long. An official from Trinidad held that Trinidadians, if given equal opportunity, can compete with any North American company in the service sector. Guyanese officials were optimistic of that country's ability to compete with other free trade areas, now that the Guyanese dollar has been substantially devalued. Contrary to expectations, there were no perceptible ideological differences between political parties in some MDCs. Jamaica's Peoples National Party is currently pursuing similar policies to that of its predecessor, the Jamaica Labour Party. The same holds true for Barbados.

The LDCs in contrast are far less optimistic on the subject of free trade and the EAI. "The free trade component is not on because we have little to offer and our productive sector is not developed" said Gloria

Payne, a Permanent Secretary in the Grenada government.[37] Although a big supporter of OECS union and the current multilateral framework agreement, Prime Minister John Compton of St. Lucia recently suggested that "foreign investors bent on paying St. Lucians low wages should relocate to places like Haiti."[38] Eugenia Charles, Prime Minister of Dominica, has also expressed concern that the islands of the Eastern Caribbean may be expected to open up their markets before they have fully developed their developmental infrastructure.[39] So, although CARICOM countries have signed a multilateral framework agreement which many view as a prelude to eventual free trade, there is no consensus on the free trade issue. Thus, any cracks in the fragile multilateral coalition could jeopardize the region's bargaining position in the future.

Lack of consensus among the region's elite is only one part of the concern facing the region's leaders. Views on free trade and the need for Caribbean unity have not yet filtered down to the masses. Joan Purcell says: "The debate regarding free trade has not reached down to the people, it is still being debated between the academics and the politicians." Purcell holds that this is the case with many issues such as the Common External Tariff (CET). "If these issues are not debated among the people, when they are implemented the people believe it is not in their interest.

---

[37] Conversation with Gloria Payne, Permanent Secretary, Prime Minister's office, Grenada: August 2, 1991.

[38] See Caribbean Update vol 7, No. 8, Sept. 1991, p.17.

[39] See Guest Opinion in Caribbean Action, Dec. 1990, pub. Caribbean/Central America Action, Washington, p.4.

That happens a lot in Caribbean politics. The politicians may be good but if the debate is not taken to the people, the people don't feel that the policy relates to them."[40] Mrs. Purcell also spoke on the subject of unity:

> The West Indian Commission, once again, is combined of a group of high-powered intellectuals. They came around and spoke to a few people but we have not been able to capture the minds and imaginations of our people regarding the integration process because integration is articulated as an economic process. But integration is not just an economic process. It has to be a cultural experience and those elements are often left out. The man in the street wants to know how the widening of the market and the question of unity will affect their lives. So there must be an element in integration that captures the *esprit de corps*. The real life of the integration experience is the cultural component.

A similar view is shared by Dr. Rosina Wiltshire-Brodber, a well-known political scientist. In a paper presented to commemorate the first ten years of CARICOM, Dr. Wiltshire-Brodber points to the role which Caribbean people themselves have played and have to play in the integration process. Furthermore, she proposes the view that there is a strong integration movement within the Caribbean "with points of fragility and many points of strength."[41] Wiltshire-Brodber suggests that the core

---

[40] Discussion with Mrs. Purcell, Grenada, July 31, 1991 [40]1241

[41] See "A Wholistic Theory of Regional Integration" in Ten Years of CARICOM: Papers presented at a Seminar on Economic Integration in the

of the integrated Caribbean region consists of Grenada, St. Vincent and Trinidad and Tobago "which are linked together by strong political, economic and social bonds fuelled by the historic and ongoing massive population movement existing among these countries." According to Wiltshire-Brodber, it is not only the fact of population movements between those countries which is responsible for this 'strong integration movement.' Other contributing factors have been the small size of the states concerned, their close proximity to each other and to a great extent their common racial, language, cultural and historical heritage.

While I am in general agreement with Dr. Brodber, I would include Barbados as another important unit in any future regional integration movement. Barbados has, in recent times, become the hub or meeting place for many of the Caribbean's educated elite population, largely due to the stability of the island and its relatively well functioning infrastructure, as well as the growing number of West Indians that have chosen to locate in Barbados. The island is also small and close to most of the smaller states in the eastern Caribbean. It has become quite common, for example, for people to travel from St. Vincent and the Grenadines, Dominica, St. Lucia or Grenada to have medical treatment in Barbados. Another significant unit would be, as in the past, the University of the West Indies, which now has a campus in Barbados. As it provides higher education to the region, it promotes regional culture and identity.

Another reason for including Barbados is that political relations between Grenada and Trinidad have been strained since the early eighties

---

Caribbean held in Bridgetown, Barbados, July 1983, p. 192.

when the Bishop regime ruled in Grenada. The government of Trinidad and Tobago did not support Grenada's revolutionary government nor the US invasion. A lot of West Indians perceive this attitude as arrogant and, as a result, Trinidad and Tobago are not as closely associated with the other islands. On the other hand, Barbadians pledged financial and moral support to their Grenadian neighbours. This helping-hand approach continues to be remembered by nationals of the 'Spice Island.' In contrast, Trinidad imposed visa requirements on all Grenadians for 'security reasons,' an act that appears to have done much to cool relations to the present.

It could be argued that other islands as well share much with countries like Grenada and St. Vincent, principally those within the Windward Islands group like St. Lucia and Dominica. In addition to their small size and proximity, St. Lucia and Dominica shared a number of institutions with Grenada and St. Vincent and the Grenadines during the colonial period, as they do today under the OECS. They are also essentially economically dependent on agriculture, having no mineral resources to speak of.

According to Wiltshire-Brodber, Jamaica, at the outer periphery of the English-speaking Caribbean, is the "weakest link in the integrative chain." However, it seems to have changed its position on the Framework agreement and is now actively participating in CARICOM, under the Chairmanship of Michael Manley, Jamaica's Prime Minister. Manley has recently proposed a tourism conference to integrate tourism for the region. But the way towards greater regional integration is still fraught with obstacles.

Any effort to promote greater regional integration through labour mobility could backfire. Increasing unemployment levels in most CARICOM countries in the 1990s, coupled with the competition of cheaper labour in Mexico and other competing Caribbean and Latin American countries, could make organized labour in the region oppose greater labour mobility. One of the inconsistencies of this stand is that organized labour is unlikely to oppose free trade. Peggy Antrobus and colleagues point to a number of reasons why organized labour in the Caribbean is unlikely to strenuously oppose free trade:[42] They are traditionally tied to political parties, unions have been penetrated by pro-capital US institutions, there is a lack of unions in the growing sectors in which women are employed, and unions have been unable to organize the growing informal sectors. Moreover, although labour organizations such as the Caribbean Congress of Labour (CCL) are sceptical of the benefits of export-processing zones and have argued in favour of better rights for workers in those zones, they have been "most timid in challenging what appears to be the unwritten understanding between governments and foreign capital that labour legislation will not be applicable in these zones."[43] Thus, Antrobus concludes that unions as well as political parties, because of their seeming inability to fill a vacuum, are increasingly being replaced by "new grassroots groups, local development organizations (LDOs), all engaged in pragmatic

[42] Deere et al. p. 97.

[43] Antrobus et al. 1990: 99.

actions to defend the rights of poor men and women opposing the austerity and sometimes repressive measures of governments."[44]

Another factor hindering the chances of integration is the severe 'brain drain' over the past years from the region to developed countries because of the inability and unwillingness of regional governments to improve the condition of basic services and to place a higher priority on the value of 'human resources'. While economic considerations have taken precedence in the regional movement over the past two decades, the political challenges still present some of the greatest obstacles in the way of unity for the CARICOM Community. With so many factors still operating against greater regional integration, one wonders just how the difficulties will be overcome. Nevertheless, the Caribbean community has been able to come together for the common good, in spite of divergent views and individual interests. This has been demonstrated by the signing of the recent Multilateral Framework Agreement between Community members and the US. The question remains, however, as to whether this 'unity' can be sustained in the months and years ahead, as we enter an increasingly more competitive and less sympathetic world environment. The thaw in East-West relations, and the growing economic difficulties in Europe, are likely to put great strain on traditional sources of aid, and Commonwealth Caribbean countries will no longer be able to use the 'threat of Communism' as a bargaining chip with developed countries. For all these reasons many people in the region are beginning to rethink the advantages

[44] Antrobus, et al., 1990 p. 101.

of greater integration efforts. As one politician recently told me "If Europe can do it with all of their diversity why can't we?"[45]

Indications are, however, that CARICOM countries still support the incremental approach. A recent poll of Trinidadians, conducted by Dr. Patrick Emmanuel, professor of politics at the University of the West Indies in Barbados, found that twenty five percent or one quarter of those polled supported the idea of political union among CARICOM countries, while the remaining sixty to seventy percent said that they would support more functional co-operation without going as far as political union.[46] Dr. Emmanuel and others believe that the results of the Trinidad poll which had a 3.5 percent margin of error, reflects an unwillingness to make any commitment to political union, particularly in the larger Caribbean countries.

Ramphal of the West Indian Commission says that "The real object of West Indian unity is to create a wider field for ambition, to make up for smallness and broaden horizons. That is what people in the Caribbean so desperately need. What they need is a change in the quality of life in which governance is a quality they respect, along with civil society."[47] Ramphal believes that "the Caribbean will be consigned forever

---

[45] Conversation with Hugh Marshall, former Trade Minister of Antigua, March, 1991.

[46] Conversation with Dr. Patrick Emmanuel, Barbados: September 22, 1991. Fifteen hundred people were polled and the margin of error was estimated at approximately 3.5 percent.

[47] Talk by Shidrath Ramphal at International Development Research Council (IDRC) office, Ottawa, Canada, May, 1991.

to the margins of the world economy if they do not unite."[48] According to Ramphal, federation, in the 50s, "was ahead of its time and its memories have retarded contemporary unity." He argues that the approach today must be one of "taking first steps first." One of these, he says, is to make freedom of movement within the region a reality. Another important step is to combat the growing problem of "cultural saturation." Some countries have as many as eighteen television channels, none of which originates in the Caribbean. This tendency is a real obstacle in the way of developing a regional identity.

The challenge for regional politicians is to find ways to capture the minds and imaginations of their people. This work can only be done by the political elite which have first to overcome the basic problem of insularity. The late Caribbean statesman and Nobel Prize winner, Sir Arthur Lewis, said that the present generation of political leaders would have to pass before any serious progress would be made towards regional integration. Many doubt that regional integration will occur without some form of extra-regional coercion.

Regional integration in the CARICOM sense has been only partially successful. The relative success of CARICOM has occurred perhaps because it has stressed economic over political concerns. However, the West Indies Federation has shown that political factors are as important as economic ones in achieving lasting unity. Many of the problems which resulted in the break up of the Federation in the mid sixties

[48] See "Caribbean States Want Stronger Ties with Canada" in the Ottawa Citizen, Sunday, June 9, 1991 p. E5.

continue to exist. Deepening and widening the process of regional integration will require that issues such as freedeom of movement, low and declining identification with the region, the regional balance of power and a lack of consensus on the part of the political elite need to be addressed.

While the benefits of the EAI remain dubious, the initiative has challenged Caribbean countries in their present state of fragmentation to respond. The EAI, along with the dramatic changes occurring in Europe, are signals which the Caribbean community can no longer ignore. The EAI and other international forces are exerting tremendous external pressure on the members of CARICOM. How this reality is conveyed to Caribbean populations by the political elite could determine the fate of the regional movement. The next chapter will demonstrate the nature of the challenge posed by a NAFTA on Caribbean countries.

Chapter 4

The Impact of a NAFTA on the Apparel Industry: A Case Study

A close examination of a particular industry will show the various factors at play and the effect that a North American Free Trade Agreement (NAFTA) will have on the region. The apparel industry will be the focus of this examination. It is an important sector because, while few Caribbean countries have textile plants, virtually all have apparel factories. For this reason this chapter will focus more on the apparel trade. Indeed, apparel assembly represents one of the few successful manufacturing attempts in most Caribbean countries and, more importantly, provides employment for a growing number of the unemployed, many of whom are women.

In the past, both the United States (US) and Canada have argued that opening the textile and apparel industries to developing countries like those of the Commonwealth Caribbean would undermine these industries in North America. However, a NAFTA could see a reduction and eventual elimination of tariffs and other rules governing the textile and apparel industries in the case of Mexico, which is still considered a developing country. What will this mean for Commonwealth Caribbean countries which currently enjoy certain tariff and quota benefits under the Caribbean Basin Initiative (CBI)? The argument posed here is that the inclusion of Mexico in the Free Trade Agreement could adversely affect the apparel industry in the Caribbean.

This chapter will begin by examining the current situation between the Caribbean and the US through the Special Access Programme and the Mexican Maquiladora programme with specific reference to the apparel trade or garment industry. Then the effect of the Canada/US FTA on apparel industry from Mexico will be discussed. This will be followed by an assessment of the effect on Caribbean apparel of the proposed NAFTA.

To date, the privileged access that Caribbean Basin countries enjoy to the US and Canadian markets excludes so-called 'sensitive' products such as textiles and garments. Although many of these countries appear not to have taken full advantage of the one-way trade advantage offered them in a variety of areas, (judged by a lack of significant increases in exports to North America), it is also true that the very items which were excluded are the ones in which the region has demonstrated a production capacity. This is apparent in the increase in garment production in some countries like Jamaica, as a result of special measures taken by the US government to facilitate both US and Caribbean apparel producers since 1986. These measures were designed to supplement the provisions of the CBI which were thought to be ineffective in promoting trade and investment. As earlier noted, while trade has increased in some untraditional sectors, the levels still remain below expectations. Most Caribbean countries require foreign investment to supplement a domestic shortage of capital for industrial development and to provide jobs for a growing number of the unemployed.

Now, Caribbean countries fear that, among other things, strict rules of origin requirements under a NAFTA will make more difficult attaining benefits afforded under the existing CBI and further complicate trade with Canada. This fear seems valid in light of a recent statement by John Weekes, Canada's chief negotiator at the trilateral negotiations. Weekes says that Canada would "ensure that the benefits of the agreement will extend only to firms producing goods in one of the three countries."[1]

Rules of origin enable the parties to an agreement to maintain different external tariffs. This is done by establishing a set percentage of value-added in the traded good that must originate in the partner country. The rules prevent third countries from shipping goods to partner countries with lower external tariff for transshipment to a partner that maintains higher tariffs against the third country's goods.[2] Rules of origin are likely to affect the apparel industry because of the special arrangements which currently exist between the US, Caribbean and Mexican governments.

The textile and apparel industry is governed by the Multi Fibre Arrangement (MFA). Since 1974 the textile and clothing trade has been regulated by the MFA which enables countries to restrict these imports by imposing quotas and tariffs if imports are believed to cause market disruptions. These measures were originally adopted to protect the North American market from competition from low-cost producers in the Far East. It was also a response to heavy lobbying from organized interests in these

---

[1] Toronto Star "Business Today: 3-way Trade Deal Aids Canada, Negotiator Says" by David Crane, June 4, 1991, p.B3.

[2] Jeffrey J. Schott, More Free Trade Areas? Washington: Institute for International Economics, May, 1989, No. 27, pp.25-26.

sectors, at a time when the rising dollar made it more difficult for Canadian and US apparel firms to compete.[3] The MFA is an exception to the National Treatment (NT) concept described in Article 111 of the General Agreement on Tariffs and Trade (GATT). NT requires that imported goods be treated no less favourably then domestically produced goods.[4] The possible elimination of the MFA is being considered in the current Uruguay Round of GATT negotiations.[5] If the MFA were to be eliminated sometime in 1992, another element would be added to the effect of a NAFTA on the apparel industry in developing countries such as the Caribbean.

The MFA was used by the US administration, rather than the powerful lobbies, to justify excluding 'sensitive' items like apparel from national treatment, when the CBI was extended to Caribbean Basin countries. It was only when the CBI appeared to be having little or no impact on the region that the US Administration made some concessions to include 'sensitive' products.

The "Special Access Programme," (SAP) was the main concession afforded Caribbean countries during the Reagan Administration. The programme was designed to increase and expand exports of US fabric and garment parts to the region, as well as to promote manufacturing and

---

[3] Marjorie Griffin Cohen, Free Trade and the Future of Women's Work, Ottawa: The Canadian Centre for Policy Alternatives (1987), p. 25.

[4] Backgrounder, 1989: 11.

[5] This round of GATT negotiations is named after Uruguay, the country where the current negotiations began.

thereby alleviate the region's economic problems.[6] The Special Access Programme for apparel, also known as TSUS 807 A, allows for negotiated Guaranteed Access Levels (GALs) for apparel items which are cut in the US and made of US fabric. These levels are higher than the quotas set by the MFA. In addition, it enables Designated Consultation Levels (DCLs) for items which were assembled from other than US-cut and-made fabric. In the absence of "market disruption," a term which refers to the injury test that has for a long time been used to limit textile and apparel imports under the MFA, GALS may be increased upon a request by the exporting country. There is also provision for automatic increases.[7]

Many Caribbean countries had hoped that Canada would have implemented a programme similar to the US 807 A, to help boost apparel sales between the Caribbean and Canada. In 1990 total garment exports to Canada from Jamaica stood at US $2.8 million as opposed to US $248 million to the US.[8] However, many now fear that a NAFTA would preclude the necessity for either US or Canadian investors to seek new off-shore investment in order to take advantage of cheaper labour. Manufacturers of apparel would have the option of moving to Mexico instead. While Canada's CARIBCAN programme precludes any special arrangement for apparel such as the 807 A programme, the Canadian

---

[6] Peter Steele The Caribbean Clothing Industry: The US and Far East Connections, Special Report No. 1147, London: (1988), p.53.

[7] Trade Opportunities for Industry, Trinidad: Government of Trinidad and Tobago, (1991), p.111.

[8] Statistics provided by the Statistical Institute of Jamaica External Trade Publications - 1986-1990.

market is still a valuable source of hard currency and trade for many Caribbean countries.

Under the SAP, US imports of apparel reached $793 million in 1989, doubling the 1986 figure from CBI countries.[9] However, as of 1989, only five Caribbean Basin countries had signed bilateral agreements enabling them to take advantage of this benefit: Haiti, the Dominican Republic, Jamaica, Trinidad and Tobago and Costa Rica.[10]

Of the two Commonwealth countries, Jamaica and Trinidad and Tobago, Jamaica has made the most advantage of the SAP. A study was done of the Jamaican apparel industry to determine the effectiveness of the SAP. It found that the industry had undergone some significant changes in the eighties.[11] In the early eighties the majority of apparel producing companies were locally owned. However, as a result of government restructuring aimed at reorienting the economy toward export manufacturing, and the adoption of large-scale advertising initiatives designed to attract foreign investment, the apparel industry is now "overwhelmingly in the hands of foreign companies producing for overseas markets."[12] While some production is still based on what is referred to as

---

[9] Hufbauer et al., p.16.

[10] Deere et al. In the Shadows of the Sun, Boulder, Colorado: Westview Press, (1990), p. 160.

[11] Catherine Hyett, The Impact of the Caribbean Basin Initiative in Jamaica and the Eastern Caribbean: An Assessment Kingston: Queens's Univ. (1989), p.40.

[12] Ibid.

"Cut, Make and Trim" (CMT), a growing proportion is now based on the assembly of pre-cut fabric imported from and reexported to the US.[13]

Before comparing the Caribbean industry to the Mexican and examining the possible effect of the NAFTA, an examination of the current status of the industry is necessary.

Between 1981 and 1987 the Caribbean Basin countries significantly expanded their garment exports to the US. A 20 percent increase was recorded in 1983 by CBI countries over that produced in 1981. A further increase of 28 percent was realised between 1984 and 1986. These increases are directly related to the SAP.[14] By far the largest CARICOM producer was Jamaica which recorded some of the highest gains in the region among CBI countries. Between 1984 and 1987 it is estimated that Jamaica's apparel exports to the US increased by 580 percent, amounting to roughly $186 million in 1987. Over half of this amount was generated by the 807 A programme.[15]

The relative success of 807 operations is attributed to the absence of notable textile industries in the region, as well as an absence of investment in integrated garment manufacturing capable of competing in the international market. The absence of a significant domestic market is thought to be one of the main reasons for this lack of investment. However,

---

[13] Ibid.

[14] USITC, Third Annual CBERA Report, p. 76.

[15] See Catherine Hyett, The Impact of the Caribbean Basin Initiative in Jamaica and the Eastern Caribbean: An Assessment, Kingston: Queen's Univ. (1989), p.40.

in the mid-1980s some Far Eastern companies began to invest for the CMT market in the US, hoping to take advantage of more favourable terms than is currently available in the Far East.[16]

As of 1987, 54 percent of new investments in the Caribbean Basin were of US origin with 24 percent originating in the Caribbean. The balance was provided by Asian firms. A breakdown of Asian investments indicates that the Dominican Republic attracted fifteen Korean and nine Taiwanese firms to its industrial parks while Jamaica attracted capital from Hong Kong.[17] Asian investments in the region have been largely influenced by rising costs of production in the Far East, as well as an experienced quota reduction to the US market for Singapore, South Korea, Taiwan and Hong Kong in 1989.[18]

The picture for direct US investments in the region differs significantly between the late seventies and early eighties and that currently recorded for the nineties. Between 1977 and 1982 the Caribbean Basin experienced a faster rate of growth in US investments and return on investments (17.4 percent) than practically any other region. However, since 1983 there has been a steady decline in US investments, with the

---

[16] See Peter Steele, The Caribbean Clothing Industry: The US and Far East Connections, Special Report No. 1147, London: The Economist Intelligence Unit, October, 1988, p.69.

[17] For more detailed information see Larry Luxner, "Asian Industries Skip P.R. as They Invest in Caribbean," Caribbean Business, 30 june 1988, pp. 1-2 in Carmen Diana Deere et al. In the Shadows of the Sun, Caribbean Development Alternatives and U.S. Policy, Boulder: Westview Press, 1990, p. 144.

[18] Ibid.

exception of some financial centres such as Bermuda, the Bahamas, and Barbados, which continued to experience steady growth. The most notable declines have been recorded for the Netherland Antilles, Belize, The Dominican Republic, Jamaica and Trinidad and Tobago. If the financial centres were to be excluded, US investments were highest in 1980 at $1.8 billion. Since then there has been a steady drop levelling out at around $900 million in 1988.[19]

The only new origin of financing for investment purposes under the CBI has been through an initiative proposed by the government of Puerto Rico. In November of 1986 the government of Puerto Rico signed a revision to section 936 of the US Internal Revenue Code which allows section 936 funds to be used to finance direct investment projects in the Caribbean, via financial and commercial institutions or indirectly through Puerto Rico's twin plant programme.[20] This initiative had an extremely slow start and has so far benefitted only a few countries in the region.

There appears to be a noticable drop in foreign investment by American companies in many Caribbean Basin countries, which many attribute to the growing US interest in Mexico. While many sectors of the Mexican economy have suffered through the economic crises of the last few years, industries in a particular region, Maquiladora, have continued to multiply and prosper. Originally established between 1956 and 1963, the Maquiladora was designed to enable US multinationals to face growing competition from Japan and Western Europe. Two new items in the US

[19] Ibid.

[20] Ibid.

tariff code - 806.30 and 807-reduced duties on imports with US components assembled or processed abroad. Indeed, the Free Trade Zones (FTZs) now in operation in the Caribbean were patterned after the Maquiladora programme. Under the programme, foreign corporations have been encouraged to establish wholly-owned subsidiaries in Mexico, as long as they agree to produce almost exclusively for export.[21]

The Maquiladora industry, accounting for almost one-third of US-Mexico two-way trade, consists of more than 1,500 plants and 400,000 workers in Mexico and is the country's second largest source of foreign exchange. Thousands of US manufacturers, employing over 100,000 workers, are involved in providing components to plants in the Maquiladora.[22] Indeed, the Maquiladora, while remaining highly controversial due to its notoriously lax environmental and safety standards, has come to be considered an important part of Mexico's economy. In addition, it has allowed US firms to retain their international competitiveness.

The apparel industry is one of the leading sectors in the Maquiladora. As well, unlike the Caribbean, Mexico has a fast developing textile capacity. In February of 1988 the US and Mexico signed a new bilateral textile agreement expanding the levels of access to the US market

---

[21] Business America, "Mexico's Maquiladora Program: An Option to Retain Competitiveness," by Tim Gilman, Washington: December 4, (1989), p.13.

[22] Ibid.

and creating a Special Regime which established generous quotas for textile and apparel products assembled in Maquiladora plants from parts cut and formed in the US. These new duty-relief provisions, known as Harmonized Tariff System (HTS), increased Mexican quotas from 50 to 90 percent.[23] The Special Regime was expanded in February 1990 as part of a 1989 consultative understanding regarding trade and investment. On this occasion, the US eliminated quotas on 52 items. All other items had their quotas increased by 25 percent.[24]

Special regime categories are subject to Special Limits (SLs) or Designated Consultation Limits (DCLs). Mexico's own trade reforms together with the Special Regime have resulted in Mexico approaching its quota limits on several occasions. When apparel exports reached the full quota in 1989, arrangements were made by the US Commerce department to augment the DCLs under the Special Regime in order to accommodate additional Mexican exports to the US.[25] US actions have been a response to a number of initiatives by two successive Mexican governments to change the country's direction from an inward to an outward looking nation. These initiatives have been linked to Mexico's debt problem manifested in the early eighties and the need for foreign capital and investment. Since then, Mexico has adopted an "open for business" policy, which has included joining the GATT in 1985 and, more recently, its interest in a free trade agreement with the US and Canada.

---

[23] Hufbauer et al. p.10.

[24] Ibid. p.14.

[25] Ibid.

The apparel trade has increased substantially between the US and Mexico. Bilateral trade increased from $469 million to 41,550 million between 1985 and 1990; US exports to Mexico increased from $180 to $862 million.[26] The overall US trade balance with Mexico in the textile and apparel sectors changed from a $109 million deficit to a $174 million surplus. This turnaround was the result of a noticeable increase in the US textile trade balance with Mexico. On the other hand, during the past 5 years, the US deficit in the apparel sector has remained between $180 and $200. Mexico is now more dependent on the US market than the US market is on Mexico, exporting 91 percent of its textile and apparel goods to the US while the US imports about 64 percent of its textiles and apparel from Mexico.[27]

In spite of the advantage given CBI beneficiaries over Mexico and the expanding capacity of some CBI countries, Mexico is a significant contender in the apparel industry. In 1988 the US tariff rate on apparel imports under GALs from Caribbean Basin countries was 4.9 percent. The figure applied to similar imports from Mexico that same year was 8.6 percent. Roughly 75 percent of the value of the goods used by Caribbean exporters was derived from components made in the US as compared with 55 percent for Mexican exporters.[28] Despite these advantages Mexico is

---

[26] Ibid. 16.

[27] Ibid. p.16.

[28] Hafbauer et al. p.17.

now the second largest producer of apparel in the Central American Caribbean area, after the Dominican Republic.[29]

The creation of a NAFTA could tip the balance in favour of Mexico in a number of ways. First, a NAFTA would most likely involve extending the current rules of origin of the Canada-US FTA to include products wholly or partially manufactured in Mexico. During the Canada-US FT negotiations certain Canadian companies feared that US goods benefitting from components from the Mexican Maquiladora programme would have an advantage over their Canadian counterparts. These interests are expected to be even more forceful at the prospect of the Mexican apparel industry receiving duty-free treatment. At the same time, significant interests in Canada and the US appear determined to ensure that Mexico does not become the backdoor for Asian exports to the US, by establishing so-called "screwdriver" plants in Mexico, in other words, factories for assembly. Thus, the rules of origin respecting the apparel sector are likely to be particularly strict with respect to third-country goods. This could complicate the procedure for apparel producers in the Caribbean.[30]

In addition, Mexico has certain natural advantages that would give it an edge over the Caribbean. While wages in many Caribbean countries are currently comparable with that of Mexico, they are less

---

[29] Steele, 1988: 69.

[30] For more information on the Canada-US rules of origin see Michael Hart, A North American Free Trade Agreement; The Strategic Implications for Canada, Ottawa: Centre for Trade Policy and Law, Institute for Research on Public Policy, (1990),pp. 104-105.

rigourously enforced (see Table 1, page 108). It is doubtful whether most Caribbean governments would be willing to go as far as Mexico in order to attract foreign investment. The current Mexican government has shown that it is willing to go to great lengths to maintain worker compliance "providing soldiers and police to stifle union organization and crush strikes."[31] While Caribbean countries regard the employment opportunities presented by the apparel trade to be important in alleviating the unemployment situation, at the same time many countries recognize the limited potential of such jobs created in this sector, particularly under the 807 A regime. In the region the industry employs about 80 percent women and its wages are notoriously low, requiring minimal skill since much of the work involves assembling pre-cut imported fabric. Thus governments regard this sector as a first step in the manufacturing process which should lead to greater job transformation in the future.[32] Ideally, Caribbean countries would prefer to negotiate reasonable terms for workers in the apparel trade rather than allow firms to operate without restrictions.[33]

Transportation is another area in which Mexico has a clear advantage over the Caribbean. Mexico has a land border with the US, allowing cheaper overland transportation. In contrast, Caribbean countries

---

[31] Also see the Ottawa Citizen "Police Torture Still Routine Amnesty Says" by Louise Crosby, Ottawa: Wednesday, September 18, 1991, p.A9.

[32] Talk by Mrs. Beverley Anderson-Manley, advisor to the Jamaican government on Women's Affairs and Jamaica's representative to the United Nations Commission on Women, Ottawa: September 21, 1991.

[33] Conversation with Mrs. Joan Purcell, Minister of Tourism, Government of Grenada, Grenada, August, 1991.

TABLE 1

HOURLY WAGES IN THE CARIBBEAN, 1991 (in US$)

Haiti	.58
Dominican Republic	.75
Dominica	.81
Grenada	.83
Belize	.85
Jamaica	.85
St. Lucia	.90
Montserrat	.92
St. Kitts	1.00
St. Vincent	1.07
Trinidad-Tobago	1.35
Barbados	1.83
Antigua	2.06
Netherlands Antilles	2.23
Bahamas	2.50
U.S. Virgin Islands	4.50
Puerto Rico	4.85

Source: Reprinted by The Bobbin magazine November 1991, Bobbin Blenheim Media Corp., Columbia, SC.

1) Hourly wages include fringe benefits; the data are for semi-skilled labor in export processing industries.

have to depend on sea or air transport, both of which are more costly and somewhat less efficient. Most of the region's cargo is currently shipped through Miami or New York. Recent problems concerning drug trafficing between Jamaica and the US has served to complicate trade between that island and the US even further. This type of complication can hardly be afforded by Caribbean countries, so dependent on reliable transportation. The absence of direct sea transportation and the high cost of air freight is particularly acute with respect to trade with Canada, which is another important trading partner for the Caribbean.[34]

Another factor favouring Mexico is its lower energy costs. Trinidad and Tobago and to a lesser extent Barbados are the only CARICOM countries with energy resources. Mexico's oil industry gives it a competitive advantage in the production of synthetic fibres such as polyester textured yarn and worsted spun acrylic yarn.[35] This potential could influence the activities of multinational industries involved in these sectors. In the long term, a combination of additional capital and more modern technology could offer possibilities for increasing production in Mexico's textile and apparel industries. Mexico also benefits from a sizable domestic market, with a current population of just over 80 million which is expected to grow substantially over the next decade. In contrast, the

---

[34] Conversation with Montreal garment producer "Strands Ltd." September 27, 1991.

[35] See Canada and a Mexico-United States Trade Agreement (Working Paper) Ottawa: Department of Finance, Canada, July, 1990, p.11.

current population of all Caribbean countries is just over 40 million. A NAFTA would increase Mexico's market size to over 360 million.

The Canada-US FTA has already had an impact on Canada's apparel industry. Slumping sales are being blamed on "the recession, rising taxes and increased US competition resulting from the 1989 Canada-US Free Trade Agreement." [36] In addition, Canadian apparel producers argue that the Canada-US free trade benefits US apparel manufacturers more because of a "rules of origin" clause. This clause specifices that garments qualify for tariff reduction, as long as the fabric from which they are made is also produced domestically. Unlike US clothing manufacturers, most Canadian-made apparel manufacturers use imported fabrics.[37]

A NAFTA would eliminate advantages of the CBI and the natural advantages of Mexico would put it in a better position. Increased Mexican competition could have both short and long-term effects for Caribbean countries. A recent report on the prospects for North American free trade concludes that in the short term "Caribbean Basin countries would be adversly affected as the Mexican regime became as favourable" as that of Caribbean countries.[38] Furthermore, "In the long run, free trade with Mexico could prompt the United States and Canada to take a less

---

[36] See Maclean's "Riches to Rags" Toronto: Maclean Hunter December, (1991), p.54.

[37] See Jan Ravensbergen and Shirley Won, "Trade Talks Worry Some Industries" Montreal Gazette, February 6, 1991.

[38] Ibid.

liberal view on freer trade with other developing countries." [39] Other studies which have relied on econometric models to estimate the effects of a NAFTA reach the conclusion that, "with free trade, Mexican exports might increase by as much as $460 million."[40] Some trade experts suggest that these figures are conservative and that Mexican exports of textiles and apparel could indeed reach $3 billion in 10 years, an export gain of over $2 billion.[41] If these predictions are correct, and the Mexican apparel industry is successful in swamping the North American market, Caribbean countries have just cause for concern.

Some analysts speculate that the effect of the NAFTA on the Caribbean can be compared to the effect of the Canada-US FTA on the Canadian apparel industry. The Canadian apparel industry is similar in that it uses mostly imported fabric, although it is more technically advanced than that of the Caribbean. Other points of similarity are that transportation in Canada is more costly and the domestic market is smaller.

The Caribbean's disadvantage vis-à-vis Mexico would be reduced somewhat if the MFA were to be phased out in the current GATT Uruguay round of negotiations. The MFA is one of the issues on the current agenda and expectations are that its provisions will be reduced within the

---

[39] Gary Clyde Hufbauer, Jeffrey J. Schott and Lee L. Remick, "Prospects for North American Free Trade: Textiles and Apparel," unpublished paper, 1991, p.19.

[40] See the KPMG-Peat Marwick model in chapter 3, table 3.6 of Prospects for North American Free Trade by Gary Clyde Hufbauer et al. (unpublished draft), 1991.

[41] Hufbauer et al. (1991), p.21.

next few years. If the MFA were to be eliminated, other developing countries like the Caribbean would gain from reduced quotas and tariffs in apparel and textile products. Nevertheless, Caribbean countries face an uphill challenge in the apparel sector and possibly other sectors as well, as a result of a NAFTA.

The NAFTA can be expected to have an impact on other industries, similar to the apparel industry. In addition to apparel, the industries most likely to be affected are some fruit and vegetables and tourism. Mexico's climate enables fruit and vegetables to be grown year round, like that of the Caribbean. Before free trade Mexican and Caribbean fruit had to compet with fruit from states like Florida and California, where winter frost is an important factor. However, transportation costs, along with other advantages resulting from a free trade deal, are likely to increase Mexico's advantage in this important sector, in relation to Caribbean countries.

Tourism, is another industry which could face added competition from the added attention Mexico is receiving. In 1989 the tourist industry earned in excess of $7000 million for Caribbean countries and was considered one of the fastest growing industries. [42] The industry has important links with a variety of industries like construction and agriculture. Thus, a decline in tourists and/or tourism related investment

---

[42] United Nations, "The Evolution of Services in Caribbean Economies 1990-1989: Some Reflections on Past Performance and Prospects for the Future, with Special Emphasis on Tourism Services" (Trinidad: United Nations,Economic Commission for Latin America and the Caribbean (ECLAC), March 1st, 1991), pp. 8-9.

from North America to the Caribbean in favour of Mexico, would be felt by Caribbean countries.

The combination of low wages, lower transportation and energy costs, added to the prospect of reduced tariffs under a NAFTA would create an investment advantage for Mexico in the apparel sector (see Table 2, page 114). The Caribbean may be expected to lose some business because it would be cheaper to produce in Mexico. The loss would be felt more acutely by large apparel producers such as Jamaica which have benefitted the most from US investment.

The apparel industry has made a significant contribution to the economy of countries like Jamaica. In 1989 the industry employed some 23,000 people. As in other Caribbean countries, some 95 percent of those employed are women. The largest FTZ in Jamaica is the Kingston Export Free Zone which expanded from 200 employees in 1981 to 15,000 in 1989.[43] In addition, income generated from apparel exports rose from $26 million to $50 million between 1984 and 1985.[44] The US market accounted for 87 percent of Jamaica's garment exports in 1990, 58 percent of which fell under the 807 outward processing programme. Total garment exports from Jamaica to the US for 1990 stood at US $248 million.[45]

The loss is likely to be felt less acutely in the smaller countries. While the loss of new investment would affect jobs in the smaller countries, the loss may not be so significant, because workers in the smaller islands

---

[43] Hyett, 1989:41.

[44] Ibid.

[45] Statistics provided by JAMPRO International Operations, July22, 1991.

Table 2
Investment Incentives in the Caribbean, 1986

	Free Trade Zones	Tax Holiday	Import Duty Exemption	Profit Repatriation	Double Tax Relief
Antigua-Barbuda	—	10 - 15 yrs.	on raw materials & machines	no restrictions	—
Dominica	planning export processing zone	10 - 15 yrs.	on raw materials & machine for export production	almost no restrictions	granted
Dominican Republic	4 export processing zones: 2 industrial parks under construction	8 - 20 yrs.	granted	no restrictions	granted
Grenada	industrial park under construction	10 - 15 yrs.	no restrictions if from CARICOM sources	no restrictions	granted
Jamaica	2 export processing zones: 1 to begin operations	5 - 10 yrs.	granted	no restrictions	granted
St. Lucia	yes [1]	10 - 15 yrs.	—	some restrictions on nonresidents	granted
St. Vincent-Grenadines	1 industrial park, another planned	10 - 15 yrs.	granted	no restrictions	granted
Trinidad-Tobago	—	—	granted	no restrictions	granted

Source: Caribbean/Central American Action, *Country Profiles* (Washington, D.C.: C/CAA, 1986)

1) Number of free trade zones or export processing zones not reported
- Information not reported

are harder to find.[46] Countries like St. Kitts are currently losing people from the garment industry to better paying sectors like tourism and construction. Although the apparel industry is valued for the jobs it provides in the region, the industry faces competition from other industries in some of the smaller territories. Some countries like St. Lucia, which are presently experiencing a three-way boom in tourism, bananas and manufacturing exports, are actually experiencing some labour shortages which could, in the long term, affect some of the enclave industries. The apparel industry may have to raise its wage rates in order to compete with industries like tourism, in order to attract employees. However, rises in real wages without corresponding increases in productivity could jeopardise the competitiveness of the industry in some countries.[47] The apparel industry in the smaller countries is currently experiencing minimal growth so even if some garment industries are lost to Mexico some other industries are likely to benefit.[48] Thus, the effect is not likely to be as great as in the case of the larger islands.

In anticipation of the difficulties facing the region, a number of proposals are being considered on behalf of and by Caribbean countries. Regional politicians have asked the US government to "propose to Canada

---

[46] Hart conversation, October, 1991.

[47] For more on the long-term prospects of the smaller territories see Long-Term Economic Prospects of the OECS Countries, Washington: Document of the World Bank (Caribbean Division) Report No. 8058-CRG, February 15, 1990, p.91.

[48] Conversation with Mr. Aubrey Hart, Trade Commissioner, Organization of Eastern Caribbean States, Ottawa: October 15, 1991.

that the Canada-US free trade area be expanded to include common rules of origin to allow CBI content to count towards eligibility for duty free treatment, even though they enter the US duty free."[49] Other measures which have been suggested include the structuring of special transitional mechanisms designed to protect fragile Caribbean economies. It would be reasonable for these mechanisms to place special emphasis on retraining women who are the ones most likely to be affected if cut backs were to occur. At a recent regional conference organized to discuss the NAFTA one delegate thought it necessary to explain what he called the: "Apparent inconsistencies which exist between the enactment of the CBI and the negotiation of a FTA with Mexico, and to eliminate any initial conceptions that US economic policy towards the Caribbean Basin has fallen victim to the interests of a larger market."[50]

For their part Caribbean countries need to undertake a number of initiatives. These include greater integration of the apparel industry within the region (to make it more profitable to set up plants), to rationalize investment incentives, and improve the competitiveness of the apparel sector by focusing on training human resources and upgrading technology. Caribbean countries should attempt to avoid the environmental problems that have plagued Mexico's Maquiladora industries.

---

[49] See Elliott Murphy, "The Enterprise for the Americas Initiative" Antigua: Organization of Eastern Caribbean States (OECS), July, 1991.

[50] See remarks by Amadeo I.D. Francis, Deputy Secretary of State for International Relations of the Commonwealth of Puerto Rico at the San Antonio Conference on Mexico sponsored by Caribbean/Latin American Action, Hilton Palacio Del Rio Hotel, San Antonio, Texas, April 11, 1991, p.6.

The combined effect of more favourable duty treatment for Mexico and eroding quotas for CBI exports could result in "disinvestment or loss of new investment in the critical apparel sectors."[51] The policy reasons for extending special concessions to Caribbean Basin countries still pertains. Economic and political stability in the region will not be inhanced by a loss of investment in the important apparel sector. There will be a need for more assistance in direct investment.

Creating more incentives for investors to invest in the region should be a priority, along with greater access to the North American market for sectors like apparel. Caribbean countries pose no threat to the North American industry because the volume produced in the region is too small. However, no matter how liberal the arrangement is, if there is not the investment and growth, the region will not be able to take advantage of market access.

---

[51] Frederick Brooks, "Maximizing the Benefits of North America Free Trade" Statement by Frederic H. Brooks, President, Caribbean/Latin American Action to the Subcommittee on Trade, Washington: 1991, pp. 4-5.

Chapter 5

Facing the Challenge of the NAFTA: Some Conclusions

The hypothesis proposed at the beginning of this study was that the twin effect of a North American Free Trade Agreement (NAFTA) and the Enterprise for the Americas Initiative (EAI) had the potential to seriously undermine existing trading agreements between the United States, Canada and the Commonwealth Caribbean countries, as well as have negative implications on their socio-political development.

Analysis of the theory of free trade, undertaken in chapter 1 with particular reference to the Canada-US free trade agreement, revealed problems in adapting the classical theory to contemporary conditions. The theory was found to be deficient in a number of important areas, such as the politics of free trade. It was noted that, although one-way free trade had been extended to Caribbean countries under the CBI and CARIBCAN by the US and Canada respectively, these agreements had not included important sectors in which Caribbean countries enjoyed a 'comparative advantage.' The implementation of a NAFTA is likely to be more challenging to Caribbean countries than its precursor, the Canada-US FTA.

In recognition of the challenges facing Caribbean and Latin American countries, the US has proposed to extend the NAFTA to the

Caribbean and Latin America through the EAI. The programme, which has three main components, trade, investment and debt relief, was found to favour the more developed countries in the region and to make little or no allowance for any of the smaller weaker economies. Like previous initiatives, the EAI was found to provide few new solutions to the problems faced by the region. It would also impose an agenda which stresses private enterprise at the expense of public sector programmes and thus neglecting to address the problems of the majority of the islands. Discussion with islanders revealed that, despite its apparent inadequacies, Caribbean countries appear willing to endorse the initiative, mainly for a variety of political considerations.

It has been suggested that the Caribbean had three options to pursue: independence; regional integration; or satellite status, such as Cuba's relations with the Soviet Union.[1] However, Cuba's uncertain future due to changes in world economic relations and the realignment of political forces indicates that the third option is no longer viable. Indeed, the future of the first option is just as doubtful since most Caribbean countries remain dependent on foreign assistance despite nearly three decades of independence.[2] Thus, the region appears to have been left with only one viable option.

[1] Jennifer Hosten-Craig, "CARIBCAN: An Analysis and Alternative Solutions," Ottawa: (1989), unpublished paper for Carleton University.

[2] First Progress Report of the West Indian Commission, Barbados: 1991, introduction.

In order to test the validity of the hypothesis which was the basis of this study, an examination of the apparel industry was undertaken. The apparel industry was one of the sectors excluded from the CBI and CARIBCAN programmmes. It was found that significant growth had occurred in the apparel (garments) industry as a result of two special arrangements between the US administration and the governments of the Caribbean and Mexico. Both of these agreements are likely to be adversely affected by a NAFTA. It was further concluded that Mexico would benefit significantly from the reduction of tariffs and quotas and that those alterations under a NAFTA would erode the special preferences currently enjoyed by Caribbean Basin countries. In addition, Mexico's increased attractiveness vis-à-vis the Caribbean could result in drawing new investment away from the region. If the Caribbean is to maintain or better its position, it will have to persuade its trading partners to extend to it the same benefits as Mexico. It was felt that the possibility of this occurring is greater if the region takes a united position in its negotiations with NAFTA countries.

Among the political considerations discussed in chapter 3 is the lack of progress made by English-speaking members of the Caribbean Community (CARICOM) towards regional integration. Although some progress has been made by CARICOM since its implementation in 1973 in areas of functional cooperation, CARICOM has failed to implement measures designed to deepen the process of regional integration. Many of the obstacles in the way of greater cooperation and a regional identity are some of the same political problems that caused the break-up of the original federation. Vision and political will are required to overcome these difficulties and it is up to regional politicians to set the agenda and work creatively towards this goal. Although the options for the region appear to be shrinking, politicians are still reluctant to sacrifice national for regional goals and this makes the goal of regional integration still appear as an unattainable dream for many.

In chapter 3 some of the political obstacles in the way of regional integration were delineated; the view expressed here is that regional integration should be considered as a 'strategy' to combat the many challenges which presently confront the region. These challenges include the formation of mega markets or economic blocs in Western Europe in 1992, the NAFTA, and the increasing prosperity of Asian countries, which could also evolve into a union with Japan. These developments may be expected to have an impact on the region's future relations with its major trading partners and credit sources in European and North American countries.[3] The formation of trading blocs threatens to increase the competition to Caribbean countries by affording other developing countries like Mexico similar and, in some cases, better access to markets in industralized countries, at a time when the region faces a myriad of economic concerns.

The increasing democratization of Eastern Europe, along with the diffusion of tensions associated with the Cold War, is likely to make the "threat of Communism" passé in the region and shift the attention of the US

[3] CARICOM documents, April, 1991.

from strategic political to strategic economic issues.[4] Indeed, Caribbean countries are already having to compete with East European countries for aid as the need to bolster the economies of Eastern Europe has taken on an added urgency. Thus, assisting a group of Caribbean countries in their development goals is becoming less of a priority for many of the region's traditional benefactors.

Many regard the NAFTA as a US response to the formation of a European single market. The US appears to have a double-barrelled strategy; on one hand, to consolidate a strong Western hemisphere grouping, and on the other, to put pressure on the countries of Europe via GATT negotiations to liberalize their own markets, particularly in sectors like agriculture, by raising the spectre of a "fortress North America." In addition, the US hopes to combat the growing Japanese/East Asian challenge by combining US capital with Canada's resources and Mexico's cheap labour to "take on Europe and Asian competition in the global market."[5]

Deciding where the Caribbean fits in all this is not easy. "The consideration for the Caribbean in the EAI is like an apostrophe - an afterthought. Even Latin America is not central to US thinking. The US is more interested in tying up Mexico in a free trade zone."[6] A Jamaican

---

[4] CARICOM Document, "Regional Response to the Bush Proposal: Enterprise for the Americas," Guyana: CARICOM Secretariat, April, 1991.

[5] "Business Groups Favour a Deal: Labour Opposed" by Eric Beauchesne in Montreal Gazette, February 6, 1991, p. ?

[6] Conversation with George Brizan, Minister of Finance, Government of Grenada, July 31, 1991.

diplomat described the situation of the Caribbean vis-à-vis Washington this way: "We don't have the clout in Washington and our economies are very small" [7]

And what about Canada-Caribbean relations in this so-called New World Order? This relationship has long been described as "special," dating back to the Colonial period when trade between Eastern Canada and the region was at its height. In that period Caribbean rum and molasses was exchanged for Canadian salt fish and lumber. In 1990 the special relationship was recognized when the Mulroney government forgave the Commonwealth Caribbean's debt to Canada. However, merchandise trade between the region and Canada continues to be lower than either Canada or the Caribbean deem acceptable. One exception is in the area of services, which is estimated to be substantially higher than originally thought.[8] There are over 200 Canadian banks in CARICOM countries and many Canadian companies provide a wide variety of services, including telecommunications and road works. Despite the one-way free trade provisions of CARIBCAN, its exclusions are now more controversial than ever in light of the proposed NAFTA. Caribbean countries recognize that Canada's own domestic agenda, namely Quebec and the US-Canada free trade deal, have limited its ability to focus outward.

[7] Interview with Jamaican diplomat, Ottawa: September 26, 1991.

[8] This conclusion is based on recent estimates provided by the Trade Division of the Department of External Affairs, Caribbean Division, October, 1991.

It is in this context that the regional integration strategy appears most viable. First, regional integration should serve as a strategy to enable the region to face the world coherently.[9] Although regional integration by itself is not considered a panacea, it does help to focus attention on the area and strengthens the region's bargaining position.

Secondly, other efforts must be made to strengthen existing ties with European countries. The European community has been one of the largest sources of foreign aid, trade and development assistance to the region. However, there is a growing realization that Europe's needs currently coincide with that of developing countries. This realization is particularly hard for the LDCs of CARICOM which continue to benefit the most from ties with European countries. Many Caribbean analysts believe that the Lomé agreements, which have been negotiated between European countries and the Africa, Caribbean and Pacific group of countries, is the model which should inform other trade and development agreements between developed and developing countries.

Thirdly, the Caribbean must seek to enter the EAI as one bloc to ensure that the interests of all states receive maximum consideration. A hopeful start has been made by CARICOM countries to date and indications are that the message that unity equals strength is being finally taken seriously. Initiatives such as a plan to promote tourism in the region is one example of what many hope is a new awareness of the region's own potential. In addition, serious attention must be given to the present

[9] Conversation with Dr. Francis Alexis, Minister of Legal Affairs, and Attorney General, Government of Grenada, Grenada: July 31, 1991.

effectiveness of the CARICOM Secretariat. A number of reports have pointed to the need to give teeth to the decisions which are reached by Heads of Government at CARICOM meetings, many of which are never acted upon.[10]

Fourthly, the region must identify and cultivate new friends, especially in Latin America and the Far East. Relations with Venezuela, one of the closest Latin American countries, have been growing stronger for some years now. Most CARICOM countries currently have Venezuelan centres which are actively involved in promoting the culture and language of that country. Indeed, that country's one-way extension of free trade to CARICOM countries in 1991 is another indication of its willingness to build on its cultural and geographical closeness. Other countries such as the Dominican Republic, which now enjoy observer status in CARICOM, are drawing closer to the regional subgrouping in a number of trade-related areas and there is increasing speculation that before long Cuba will be joining the ranks of Caribbean countries in a substantial way. Taiwan, South Korea and Hong Kong have also shown interest in the investment potential of the region and in turn Caribbean countries are beginning to recognize the potential of the Far East.

At the regional level the spectre of free trade challenges Caribbean countries to coordinate their efforts in developing both human

---

[10] The Caribbean Community in the the 1980's, Report by a Group of Caribbean Experts, Barbados: CARICOM Secretariat, (1981). Also see To Be A Canoe, Presentation by the Chairman of the West Indian Commission Sir Shridath Ramphal to the Twelfth Meeting of the Conference of Heads of Government of the Caribbean Community, Basseterre, 2 July 1991, p.16.

and other resources, with particular emphasis on practical education and training. It is only through effective management of the region's minimal resources with the highest priority given to the region's greatest resource, human resources, that higher levels of achievement and competitiveness will be achieved. Numerous studies point to the need to develop a regional strategy which links tourism with the agricultural sector. This can be achieved by diversifying agriculture and by rationalization of the region's industries, with greater emphasis on the growing of fruits and vegetables for home consumption and export. Efforts to develop the tourist sector should focus on regional culture and attitudes. There is a general consensus that the region should not seek so much to compete with countries like Mexico as to identify specific niches in areas such as the service sector. Data processing is one of the industries which is especially well suited to the Commonwealth Caribbean, which has an absolute advantage over Mexico in its wide use of the English language as the language of work. In this regard, notable success has already been achieved by Jamaica, Trinidad and Tobago, Barbados and Grenada and evidence suggests that other countries in the region are actively pursuing this and other venture opportunities. The region will need to step up its marketing and lobbying efforts in order to attract interest, capital and investment to the region in the face of a more competitive international environment.

While Caribbean countries in the 1990s are more in step ideologically with Washington than they were in the late seventies and early eighties, no collective consensus has been declared in this regard. Jamaica and Guyana are still considered to be in a state of flux, with remaining elements of support for left-wing policies. This could add to the other political problems in achieving deeper regional integration.

The above discussion makes clear that there are no simple solutions to the problems experienced by Caribbean countries. The Free Trade model is unlikely to provide immediate solutions for Caribbean countries faced with the fundamental problems of small size and limited resource bases.[11] The Caribbean has never been under greater pressure for a regional approach than it is in the 1990s as it faces a rapidly changing international environment. Coming together in a timely way could strengthen the Caribbean's position but this will depend on a great deal of political will and initiative at the regional level. Some people believe that, until the economic situation of most Caribbean countries improves to an acceptable level of development, Caribbean politicians will continue to take a short-term individualist position rather than a long-term view of regional integration.

[11] Interestingly enough this point is also made by Carla Hills, chief negotiator of the US negotiating team in the trilateral negotiations now proceeding between the US, Canada and Mexico.

Selected Bibliography

Agreement Between the Caribbean Community ("CARICOM") and the Government of the United States of America (US) Concerning CARICOM-US Council on Trade and Investment, Washington: CARICOM Document, July 22, 1991.

Allard, Christian. "Mexico for Sale: Gringos Welcome" in Canadian Business, Toronto: November, 1990.

Axline, W. Andrew. Caribbean Integration: The Politics of Regionalism. New York: Nichols Pub. Co., 1979.

Beckford, George and Girvan, Norman. Development in Suspense: Selected Papers and Proceedings of the First Conference of Caribbean Economists. Jamaica: Friedrich Ebert Stiftung, 1989.

Boatswain, Anthony. "An Economic Perspective: Attitude and Development" in Business Eye Grenada: Business Eye Int. Ltd., February/March, 1991.

Brooks, Frederick, "Maximizing the Benefits of North America Free Trade" Washington: Caribbean/Latin American Action, February, 1991.

Bush, George. Remarks Announcing the Enterprise for the Americas Initiative, Washington: Presidential Documents, 26, No. 16, June 27, 1990.

Business America. Washington: April 25, 1988.

----------------. "Mexico's Maquiladora Program: An Option to Retain Competitiveness" by Tim Gilman, Washington: December 4, 1989.

Canada. Backgrounder: "Canada-US Free Trade Agreement" Ottawa: Library of Parliament, January 27, 1988.

------. "Canada and a Mexico-United States Trade Agreement" (Working Paper), Ottawa: Department of Finance, Canada. July, 1990.

------. Royal Commission on the Economic Union and Development Prospects for Canada (Macdonald Commission), Final Report, & Ottawa: Supply and Services, 1985, Vol. 1.

------. Statistics Canada. "Trade of Canada, Imports by Country," Ottawa: 1988.

Caragata, Warren. "Caribbean States Want Stronger Ties With Canada" in The Ottawa Citizen. Ottawa: June 9, 1991.

Caribbean Community (CARICOM) Secretariat. Ten Years of CARICOM: Papers Presented at a Seminar on Economic Integration in the Caribbean. Washington: Inter-American Development Bank, 1983.

Caribbean Action. Guest Opinion, Washington: Caribbean/Central American Action, December, 1990.

---------. The Caribbean Common Market: Trade Policies and Regional Integration in the 1990s. Washington: December 21, 1990.

Caribbean Update. Vol. 7, No. 8, New Jersey: Sept. 1991.

CARICOM Secretriat. "Regional Response to the Bush Proposal: Enterprise for the Americas." Guyana: CARICOM Secretariat, April, 1991.

------------. The Caribbean Community in the 1990s: Report by a Group of Caribbean Experts. Barbados: CARICOM Secretariat, 1981.

Cohen, Marjorie Griffin. Free Trade and the Future of Women's Work. Ottawa: The Canadian Centre for Policy Alternatives, 1987.

Conference Board of Canada. "Impact of Canada-US Free Trade on Commonwealth Caribbean Countries." A Report Prepared for the Department of External Affairs. October, 1988.

Crane, David. "Business Today: 3-way Trade Deal Aids Canada, Negotiator Says" in The Toronto Star. June 4, 1991.

Crosby, Louise. "Police Torture Still Routine Amnesty Says" in The Ottawa Citizen. Ottawa: September 18, 1991.

Dayal, R. and Dayal, N. "Trade Creation and Trade Diversion: New Concepts, New Methods of Measurement," Weltwirtschaftliches Archiv., Vol. 113, No. 1, 1977.

Deere, Carmen et al. In the Shadows of the Sun: Caribbean Development Alternatives and U.S. Policy. Boulder, Colorado: Westview Press, 1990.

Demas, William. "Development, Identity and Unity in the Caribbean" in WesIndian Nationhood and Caribbean Integration. Ed. David I. Mitchell, Barbados: CCC Publishing House, 1974.

Etzioni, Amitai. Political Unification: A Comparative Study of Leaders and Forces. New York: Holt Rinehart and Winston, Inc. 1965.

Gilpin, Robert. The Political Economy of International Relations, Princeton: Princeton Univ. Press, 1987.

Girvan, Norman. "Integration: A Realistic Option?" in Integration and Participatory Development, Selected Papers and Proceedings of the Second Conference of Caribbean Economists ed. Judith Wedderburn, Bridgetown, Barbados: Freiedrich Ebert Stiftung (FES) and Association of Caribbean Economists, 1990.

Griffith, Winston H. "CARICOM Countries and the Caribbean Basin Initiative" in Latin American Perspectives. Issue 64, Vol. 17, No. 1, Winter, 1990.

Hart, Michael. A North American Free Trade Agreement: The Strategic Implications for Canada. Ottawa: Centre for Trade Policy and Law, Institute for Research on Public Policy, 1990.

Hosten-Craig, Jennifer. The CBI: An Analysis and a Critique, Ottawa:Carleton Univ. Honours Thesis, 1989.

----------. CARIBCAN: An Analysis and Alternative Strategies, Ottawa: Carleton Univ. Unpublished paper, 1989.

Hufbauer, Gary Clyde, et al. "Prospects for North American Free Trade: Textiles and Apparel," Ottawa: 1991; unpublished paper.

Hyett, Catherine. "Caribcan: Canada's Response to the Caribbean Basin Initiative." Kingston: Queens Univ., 1989; unpublished paper.

----------. "The Impact of the Caribbean Basin Initiative in Jamaica and the Eastern Caribbean: An Assessment" Kingston: Queen's Univ., 1989.

Lowenthal, David. "The Social Background of West Indian Federation," in The West Indies Federation: Perspectives on a New Nation. Ed. David Lowenthal, New York: The Columbia Univ. Press, 1961.

----------. The West Indies Federation. New York: Columbia Univ. Press, 1961.

Maclean's. "Riches to Rags" Toronto: Maclean Hunter, December, 1991.

McDonald, Vincent R. "Regional Cooperation: Panacea for Self-Sustaining Growth." Paper prepared for presentation at XV Annual CSA Conference. Trinidad and Tobago: May 22-24, 1990.

Montreal Gazette "Business Groups Favour a Deal: Labour Opposed" by Eric Beauchesne, Montreal: February 6, 1991.

-----------. "Trade Talks Worry Some Industries" by Jan Ravensbergen and Shirley Won, Montreal: Montreal Gazette, February 6, 1991.

Murphy, Elliott. "The Enterprise for the Americas Initiative." Antigua: Organization of Eastern Caribbean States (OECS), July, 1991.

Ramphal, Shridath. To Be a Canoe. Presentation to the Twelfth Meeting of the Conference of Heads of Government of the Caribbean Community, Basseterre, St. Kitts, July 2, 1991. Barbados: 1991.

Ramsaran, Ramesh. The Commonwealth Caribbean in the World Economy. London: MacMillan Pub. Ltd., 1989.

Reid, Stanley. Significance/Relevance of the Canada-US Free Trade Agreement with Particular Reference to the Caribbean: Some Perspectives. Barbados: Export Promotion Corporation Special Symposium, April 3-5, 1990.

Royal Bank of Canada. Econoscope: Free Trade Agreement: One-Year Retrospective. Montreal: January 18, 1990, Vol. 13, No. 11-12.

Russell, Francis. "Free Trade Initiative Poses Threat to Workers Jobs," Winnipeg Free Press, Winnipeg: January 26, 1991.

Schott, Jeffrey J. More Free Trade Areas? Washington: Institute for International Economics, No. 27, May, 1989.

Soviani, Mahboob Ali. The Role of Regional Development Banks in the Integrative Process of Developing Countries. A Case Study of the Inter-American Development Bank. Ottawa: Master's Thesis, Carleton Univ., 1980.

Steele, Peter. The Caribbean Clothing Industry: The US and Far East Connections. Special Report No. 1147, London: The Economist, 1988.

The Economist "World Trade: Jousting for Advantage," London: September 22, 1990.

The West Indian Independent Commission. Towards a Vision of the Future. Progress Report, Barbados: The West Indian Commission, 1991.

Thomas, Clive Y. "From Colony to State Capitalism: Alternative Paths of Development in the Caribbean." Transition 5, 1982.

Trinidad. Trade Opportunities for Industry, Trinidad: Government of Trinidad and Tobago, 1991.

U. S. Congress. Regional Brief. "US-Mexico Relations," Washington: May, 1989.

Wagenheim, Kal. Caribbean Update, New Jersey: Vol. 7. No. 8, September, 1991.

Wedderburn, Judith. Integration and Participatory Development: A Selection of Papers from the Second Conference of Caribbean Economists. Jamaica: Friedrich Ebert Stiftung (FES), 1990.

Weintraub, Sidney. "North American Free Trade, With Emphasis on US-Mexico Relations." Paper prepared for the International Studies Assoc. 24th Annual Convention, Mexico City: April, 5-9, 1983.

Whittington, Les and McIlroy, Anne. "The Flipside of Boom" in The Ottawa Citizen. Ottawa: May 5, 1991.

Wiltshire-Brodber, Rosina. "A Wholistic Theory of Regional Integration" in Ten Years of CARICOM: Papers presented at a Seminar on Economic Integration in the Caribbean. Bridgetown, Barbados: July, 1983.

World Bank. The Caribbean: Export Preferences and Performance, Washington: December, 1988.

World Bank. "Long-Term Economic Prospects of the OECS Countries," Washington: Document of the World Bank (Caribbean Division) Report No. 8058-CRG, February 15, 1990.

Yarbrough, Beth V. and Robert M. The World Economy: Trade and Finance. Chicago: The Dryden Press, 1989.

List of Persons Interviewed

All persons listed below were interviewed between January and September, 1991.

Canada

Name	Title/Company
Jock Finlayson	Vice President Business Council on National Issues
Robert Rutherford	Director/Caribbean & Central America External Affairs
David Babinsee	Senior Vice President Bank of Nova Scotia
Nick Norcott	Director Caribbean & Central America
Tom Bearss	External Affairs &International Trade
Ennio Vita Finzi	President/ Canadian Council for the Americas
Ms. Sheila Carey	Counsellor/Bahamas High Commission
Charles Robertson	First Secretary/Guyana High Commission
Bruce McFarlane Ph.D	Prof. of Sociology/Carleton Univ.
Andrew Axline Ph.D.	Chairman/Political Science/Univ. of Ottawa.
Bernard Yankey Ph.D.	High Commission/Organization of Eastern Caribbean States (OECS)
Sandra L. Baillieul Cooperation Office	Director/Canadian, Caribbean Business
Anne Wilson	Project Coordinator/Canadian Hunger Foundation
Roxane Connick Carlisle	Anthropologist/Womens Affairs specialist

Ms. Pearl Wilson	Deputy High Commissioner/Trinidad & Tobago
Sir Cameron Tudor	High Commissioner/Barbados
Senator Heath McQuarrie	Senator for Prince Edward Island
Ms. Vilms McNish	Deputy High Commissioner/Jamaica
Halina Ostrovski	Director/Canadian Council for the Americas
Ron Jervis	Director/Strands Imports Inc. (Montreal)
Dr. Anthony Payne	Senior Lecturer in Politics/Univ. of Sheffield
Paul Sutton Ph.D.	Director/Centre of Developing Area Studies/Univ. of Hull
Aubrey Hart	Trade Councillor/OECS
Ulrick Redhead	Seasonal Workers Farm Program/Toronto
Sr. Carlos Sada	Consul General of Mexico/Toronto
Mairuth Sarsfield	Past President/MATCH/Ottawa
Prof. Ed. Dossman	Director/North/South Inst.
Ewart Walters	Journalist & Editor/The Spectrum
Prof. Vincent Wilson	Prof. of Political Science/Carleton Univ.
Murray Smith	Director/Centre for Trade Policy and Law
Robert Clark	Deputy Chief Negotiator/North American Free Trade Negotiations
Pradip Shastri	Program Manager/Americas Bureau Industrial Cooperation Div/CIDA
Erik Nilsson	Senior Economist/The Bank of Nova Scotia
Dr. Alister McIntyre	Vice Chancellor/Univ. of the West Indies
Sir. Shidrath Ramphal	Chairman/West Indian Commission
Max Cameron	Prof. of International Relations/Carleton Univ.
Gordon Ritchie	Consultant/Former Free Trade negotiator

United States

S. Vanwiganbergen	Trade Economist/World Bank Group
Magda Matamoros	Trade Specialist/Interamerican Development Bank
Hugo Seltzer	Director/Interamerican Development Bank
Peter Field	Trade Specialist/US Commerce Dept.
Peter Johnson	President/Caribbean Central American Action Group
Francis Paul	Trade Councillor/Grenada Mission in Washington
Bob Dormitzer	International Trade Administration/US Commerce Dept.
Clarence Ellis	Executive Director/World Bank Group
Barbara Mireau	Trade Economist/World Bank Group
Georges Fauriol Ph.D.	Senior Fellow & Director Latin American Studies/Center for Strategic International Studies
Ms. Mary J. Wignot	Committee Member/Subcommittee House Ways & Means
Kenny Alleyne	Executive Director/Eastern Caribbean Investment & Promotion Service
Cathy Keim	Trade Officer/Canada Division/US Commerce Dept.
Ragina Vargo	Trade Officer/Mexico Division/US Commerce Dept.
David Sevigny	Advisor to Executive Director/The World Bank

Barbados

Judith Alsopp	Trade Officer/Export Development Project, CARICOM
Rudon Eversley	Reporter, Journalist/Caribbean News Agency
Wendy Sealey	Librarian/Caribbean Development Bank
Dr. Neville Duncan	Prof. Social Sciences/Univ. of the West Indies

Richard Taurel	Managing Director/RT Services Ltd.
P. A. Thompson	Chief Executive Officer/The Caribbean Assoc. of Industry and Commerce
Earle Baccus	Project Director/CARICOM Export Development Project
Donald Brice, O.J.	Director General/West Indian Commission
Peggy Antrobus	Director/Women & Development/Univ. of the West Indies
Sylvia Potvin	Counsellor(Commercial)/Canadian High Commission
Vaughn Renwick	Trade Officer/CARICOM Export Development Project
Dr. Rosina Wiltshire-Brodber	Political Scientist/Caribbean Specialist
Delisle Worrel	Director/Central Bank of Barbados
C. Frederick	Chief Economist/Ministry of Trade/Barbados Sir Neville Nichols President/Caribbean Development Bank
Dr. Patrick Emmanuel	Prof. of Political Science/Univ. of the West Indies
Earlyn Shuffler	Regional General Manager/Caribbean & Mexico/Atlantis Submarines
Patrick Carmichael	Manager, Marketing Unit/CARICOM

Grenada

The Rt. Hon. Nicholas Brathwaite	Prime Minister/Grenada
Gordon Brathwaite	Land owner & Industralist/Lanse Aux Epines
Lucie Andel	Trade Director/Ministry of Trade
Michael Minors	Director/Chamber of Commerce
Fabian Redhead	Director/Grenada Industrial Development Corporation
Hon. George Brizan	Minister of Trade/Ministry of Trade

Hon. Francis Alexis	Attorney General/Ministry of Legal Affairs
Hon. Joan Purcell	Minister of Tourism/Ministry of Tourism
Leslie Pierre	Journalist, Editor/The Grenada Voice
Ms. Neckles	Manager/Key Universal
Senator Dennis Noel	Agricultural Specialist/Ministry of Agriculture
Sister Reina LoeSac	Director/New Life Organization
Gloria Payne	Permanent Secretary/Prime Minister's Office/Former Rep. to the United Nations

Trinidad

Clyde Applewhite	Director/United Nations Economic Commission for Latin America & the Caribbean
Dr. Clayton Najab	Head of Commerce/Trinidad and Tobago Urea Co. Ltd.
Mr. Russell Austin	Communications Director/Point Lisas Development
Gary Voss	Managing Director/Lever Bros Ltd. President/Chamber of Commerce
Corrine Baptiste	Trade Specialist/External Affairs
Sonia Cuales	Social Affairs Officer/Women in Development/ECLAC
W. Kanhai	Manager, Process Engineering /Trinidad & Tobago Methanol Co. Ltd.
Prof. Norman Girvan	Director/School of Social Sciences/Univ. of the West Indies
Angela Cropper	Former Director/CARICOM
Oscar Alonzo	Chief Executive Officer/Trinidad & Tobago Export Development Corp.

Guyana

Cam Bowes	First Secretary/Canadian High Commission
Harry Murray	Taxi driver
Francis Gobin	Managing Director/Gobins Ltd.
Marjorie Rahaman	Palm Court Restaurant
Brantford Isaacs	Director/CARICOM
L.J.P. Willems	Managing Director/Willems Timber & Trading Co. Ltd.
Hayden Blades	Trade Expert/CARICOM
Ian MacDonald	Director/Guysuco Member of the West Indian Commission
Yesu Persaud	Chairman/Guyana Distillers Ltd.
Mavis Campbell	Trade Economist/CARICOM
Clive Y. Thomas	Professor of Economics/Univ. of Guyana
Magda Pollard	Director of Womens Affairs/CARICOM
C. Barker	Owner/C & D. Fashion & Tailoring Est.
Kathleen Whalen	Director/Futures Fund/Canada Dev. Project
Mike McCormack	Director/Council of Churches and Human Rights Assoc.

St. Lucia

The Rt. Hon. John	Prime Minister/Prime Minister's Compton Office
Vaughn Noel	Radio Broadcaster/Radio St. Lucia
Norman Sutherland	Director/Chris Renwick & Co.
Barry Renwick	Legal Council/OECS
Jimmy Emmanuel	Officer/OECS Secretariat
Bonnie Zephrin	Viking Traders Ltd.
Leo Clarke	Manager/Castries Apparel Ltd.
Maurice Minvielle	Vice Pres. Finance/The Windjammer Landing Co. Ltd.
Adrian Augier	Executive Director/St. Lucia Chamber of Commerce
Dr. Vaughn Lewis	Executive Director/OECS Secretariat

Mr. Severin	Permanent Secretary/Ministry of Trade
Leslie R. Clarke	Chairman/St. Lucia National Development Corp.
Ferdinand Henry	Minister for Agriculture, Lands, Fisheries and Co-operatives

Antigua

Lester Bird	Former Deputy Prime Minister
Hugh Marshall	Former Minister of Trade
Ethlyn Simon	Manager/Industrial Development Board
Gregory Renwick	Senior Economist/OECS
Lionel Boulos	Executive Director/Antigua & Barbuda Chamber of Commerce
Paul Farara	Managing Director/La Parfumerie Ltd.
Peter J. Harker	Managing Director/Sealy Mattress Co.
Brunel Meade	Industrialization Commissioner/Ministry of Trade, Industry & Commerce
J. Francois Michel	Senior Trade Officer/OECS
Percival Marie	Senior Trade Economist/OECS
Elliott Murphy	Trade Officer/OECS

Jamaica

Prof. Kari Levitt	Visiting Prof./School of Graduate Studies/Univ. of the West Indies
Anthony Hill	Permanent Secretary/Prime Minister's office
Gillian Glean Walker	Investment Advisor/Eagle Financial Network
Kelly Joyce	Senior Commercial Officer/US Embassy
Brenda Robinson	Group Director/Jamaica Promotions Corp (JAMPRO)
Anthony Barnes	Chairman/Grace (Jamaica) Ltd. Ex. President of Manufacturing Assoc.
John Cooke	Member of Jamaican Tourist Board
Sylvia Brown	Director/Information Processing Div. JAMPRO
Winsome Miller	Director Manufacturing Inds./JAMPRO

Barry Robinson	Director/Caribbean Business Managing Co. Ltd.
John Ross	Owner/John Ross & Co.
Anne Martel	Trade Commissioner/Canadian High Commission
Dorianne Wilson Smillie	Consultant/Women and Development
Senator Lucille Mair	Ministry of Foreign Affairs
Dr. Eddy Green	Director/Institute of Social and Economic Research

Mexico

Alfred Dorsett	General Manager/Caribe Bahamas Ltd.
Charles Voight	President/Haiti Petrole, S.A.
David Rodriguez M.	Owner/Originales Chac Mool
Herman Hoppenstedt	International Sales Manager/Vitro Vidrio Plano
Lic. Fernando Ysita	President/Central America & the Septien Caribbean Promotions in Mexico
Ambassador Hector Manuel Ezeta	Special representative to the Caribbean
Lic. Humberto Molina	Director General/National Commercial Bank
Dr. Mario Sosa Castillo Medina	Director/Bancomext